THOUGHT CATALOG BOOKS

Everything You Need To Know If You Want Love That Lasts

Everything You Need To Know If You Want Love That Lasts

SABRINA ALEXIS

Thought Catalog Books

Brooklyn, NY

THOUGHT CATALOG BOOKS

Copyright © 2016 by Sabrina Alexis

All rights reserved. Published by Thought Catalog Books, a division of The Thought & Expression Co., Williamsburg, Brooklyn. Founded in 2010, Thought Catalog is a website and imprint dedicated to your ideas and stories. We publish fiction and non-fiction from emerging and established writers across all genres. For general information and submissions: manuscripts@thoughtcatalog.com.

First edition, 2016

ISBN 978-0692722589

10 9 8 7 6 5 4 3 2 1

Cover design by © KJ Parish

Contents

Introduction

I will never forget the day Facebook introduced the news feed. It was the first day of my senior year in college. I had some time to kill before class and logged on to what was then called The Facebook. But on that day it looked different. Instead of being taken to a simple page with not much on it and having to manually search for anyone you wanted to check up on (i.e. stalk), all the information about your friends appeared right before you. *Tim added* American History X *as his favorite movie. Jessica added partying to her interests.* Whoa, this is weird! I kept scrolling, intrigued and creeped out in equal measure. Then I was sucker punched.

Amy tagged Eric in 43 photos, The Facebook obnoxiously informed me. My heart stopped. The blood drained from my face. I didn't even take a pause—I immediately started clicking. And it was worse than anything I could have imagined.

There they were, sitting on his couch making cute faces...there she was sitting on his lap outside on the deck while they grilled burgers...there they were on an adventure in the woods taking turns taking pictures of one another...and there they were lying on his bed, his arm outstretched and camera pointing down towards them (this was pre-selfie era), catching her head on his bare chest. I could barely catch my breath. This was just so wrong. Everything was *so wrong*. It wasn't supposed to go down like this.

OK, let's back up for a second. Eric and I started dating at the beginning of my junior year of college. The relationship was a disaster from the start. We met a week after he'd been dumped and he was devastated. He was also struggling in countless other areas of his life. One night his buddies convinced him to go out and party the pain away. So he got nice and liquored up and went to one of Boston's coolest bars, and that's where he met me.

There was an instant explosion of chemistry, the dangerous kind that sucks you in fast and deep before you have a chance to realize what's happening. And then you're in it and there's no way out. We ended up talking the entire night (OK, and making out a little), and I was done. Like *done.* I was powerless against the pull I felt towards him, no matter how many warning signs directed me to go the other way. I was like Alice going down the rabbit hole. *Either the well was very deep, or she fell very slowly, for she had plenty of time as she went down to look about her and to wonder what was going to happen next…*

This relationship was a testament to how irrational love can be because there was no logical reason to stay, but I did. He couldn't give me what I wanted or needed and he wouldn't even call me his girlfriend after many months of seeing each other and spending literally all our time together. He liked having me around, but always on his terms. He was sweet to me, but I never felt good enough. I always felt like a placeholder. He remained purposefully beyond my reach, claiming that he'd made a vow to never let his guard fully down after being blindsided by the breakup in his last relationship. I stopped seeing my friends, stopped pursuing my hobbies and passions, stopped being me to be there for him.

OK, you get the point. It was bad. Then after about seven

months of bad, he broke up with me. It was a very sweet kind of breakup. We cried and said we loved each other and we were sad, but we knew this needed to happen. It was for the best.

It was brutal and agonizing, but I found a way to be OK. I began to rebuild myself. I wanted to love myself again, to *like* myself again. Then I started dating a really sweet, wonderful guy named Greg. I'd actually had a crush on him when I was 16 and we both worked as counselors at a day camp. This relationship started out so healthy and normal that it was almost a shock to my system. There was no drama, no confusion, no baggage…and it felt really nice.

But then Eric came back. Even though we'd agreed to have no contact for a solid three months, it took him three weeks to break. He needed me, he couldn't live without me, he had to see me. I tried to put my foot down, I said absolutely not. But he wore me down until I agreed. I told him about Greg and he lost it, completely distraught. I reminded him that the breakup was his idea. He told me that if I'd been this confident and strong when we were together, he never would have let me go. Now what the heck was I supposed to do with that bit of information?

I tried to continue my relationship with Greg—I wanted it to work, I wanted him to make me forget all about Eric—but Eric made that impossible. He wanted me back, he begged for me back, and although I tried to resist, I was just too weak. I told Greg the whole story and though he understood, he slowly started distancing himself from me. I couldn't blame him. He told me that he'd broken up with his previous girlfriend because he thought she still had feelings for her ex, and here the poor boy was, in the exact same situation!

Then Eric and I were back on...and nothing had changed. We quickly fell back into the same patterns of a bad relationship. Neither of us was in a good place internally and we just weren't good together.

Then I went home to New Jersey for summer break while he stayed in Boston. We talked every day and had a few visits, but something was missing, something didn't feel right. I figured it was the distance and thought everything would be great in a few weeks when I returned to Boston. But then the worst thing ever happened. He didn't call me back one night. That's right. OK, maybe that seems like no big deal, but it was, because he always called me back. He always called me in general because he almost couldn't function without me.

But this night he didn't, and at around 3 AM, I just knew, I felt it in my gut. *He's cheating on me, he's with a girl right now.* The next day my suspicions were confirmed on MySpace, when a very attractive girl posted some sort of inside joke on his wall. I didn't want it to be true, but it was impossible to ignore what was right in front of me, even for someone as masterful at self-deception as I was. So I confronted him and he confirmed it. I was crushed. Obliterated. *How could he?* It didn't make any sense. He needed me. I did everything for him. I'd left Greg for him! He forced me to get back together with him! It wasn't fair and it wasn't right.

Always the optimist, I didn't think this was the end. It couldn't be. I figured he would have his little fling and as soon as I was back in Boston he would come crawling back on his hands and knees.

So I rode out the rest of the summer until I moved back to Boston to start my senior year. Then Picturegate happened.

I don't think I'd ever been more wrong about anything in my life. Never in my wildest dreams or worst-case-scenario thinking did I believe he would end up in a new relationship, and not only that, a relationship that was exactly what I'd always wanted to share with him! He fell for her hard and fast, he made it official, he publicly expressed his love, he was devoted and committed.

I was in shock…how could this be? How could I be so easily replaced? This just didn't make any sense. So I called him. I called and begged him to explain, to tell me what was happening, to tell me why. It was like talking to a distant stranger; his answers were short and cold. All the love he'd once expressed had evaporated, and I was reduced to nothing more than a nuisance, a problem on the other end of the line that he didn't want to deal with but didn't know how to get rid of. It was a sickening feeling, but I needed to know why, how, who? Who was she? What did she have that I didn't? How could he do this to me? What about what we'd had? *You said you loved me and I thought that meant something!* I pleaded for these answers, but he was a block of ice and gave me little more than "It is what it is."

Every day, more photos appeared on my newsfeed of the two of them looking so sickeningly happy. And what was worse, he actually got his act together. He got a job, broke free of his depression, was actually going places and doing things. In a few short weeks this girl was able to do something that I hadn't been able to do in a year. I knew I had to stop looking, I knew I should unfriend him, but I was just too much of an emotional masochist. I couldn't get enough. And then when I finally did find the strength to unfriend him, it didn't really do much good because his profile didn't have any privacy settings.

After crying more tears than seemed possible, I just kind of turned all my emotions off. I partied my senior year away and escaped the wrenching pain in any way I could. I tried to face it, tried to tell myself it was for the best and that this too would pass…but I couldn't see a light at the end of the tunnel. The only solution for me seemed to be endless distraction, running from the pain before it could find me.

I had turned into an emotional robot. Any guys I met or talked to or kissed, I felt nothing, nada, zilch. It didn't matter how great and cute and wonderful they were, nothing registered.

Then I graduated and moved on. I moved to the Big Apple and started working as a fashion and beauty writer, living a glamorous sort of life filled with Fashion Week and parties and red-carpet events and being overworked and underpaid but still loving it. I was career obsessed, determined to make it, to succeed, to climb to the top of whatever needed to be climbed. It was a non-stop, frenetic sort of life, but no matter how busy I was the pain was still there, etched in the recesses of my mind and heart. I didn't want it to be there, but the thought of him and her and the way it all went down would sometimes catch me off guard and stab me right between the ribs. *When exactly am I going to be over this already?* And a part of me thought I would never get over it—how does one bounce back from such an emotional gutting? How does one feel again after being discarded like yesterday's news by the person loved and trusted more than anyone?

I am someone who needs to know, it's just my personality type. I always joke that if I weren't a writer I would be a detective. I just can't be satisfied until I have seen and examined all the evidence and have been able to string together a cohesive narrative of exactly what happened and why. I tried to find the answers; I tried to figure out what went wrong and why, but the real answer always evaded me.

I had a few superficial relationships after Eric, but none of them really moved me until I met Kurt. He was sexy and cool and fun and charming, and he was crazy about me. In the beginning I was too distracted to be receptive to him, but then one day it hit me that I *really* liked him. That this could really be something. Then I became afraid. All my old war wounds were suddenly raw again, and I was terrified of losing him. If he didn't text for a few hours, I would panic: that's it, he's lost interest, he's done. Then he would resurface and my fears would be instantly assuaged; hearing from him was like getting a shot of Xanax, it calmed me right down. Until the drug wore off…and then more panic. More wondering if he was really into me, if he was cheating on me, if this was going somewhere.

Then he disappeared. He vanished for a week and I was crushed. But he came back, yay! I was out at a bar one night with friends and he texted me, and I was so relieved that things were back on track that I ended up going over there at 3 AM and spending the night. I used to make really good decisions like that!

Then he disappeared *again*, only this time it was for two

weeks. But I knew he would be back, just like the last time. And he reappeared! He called me one night and I'd forgiven him for vanishing before I'd even picked up the phone...only, he hadn't meant to call me. Within a few seconds of talking it was clear that he thought he was talking to *someone else*, to some other girl, and he hung up on me as soon as he realized what he'd done. I was incredulous and refused to accept this as reality, so I tried calling him back. No answer. Then I texted him asking for an explanation. It's been almost a decade, and I'm still waiting on a response!

Right after this went down, my male roommate and some of his friends burst through the apartment, and the conversation that ensued changed my life forever. The boys saw how upset and shocked I was and made me an offer. They wanted me to go out to a party with them that night, but didn't want me to be a Debbie Downer and ruin everyone's buzz, so they gave me the floor to tell them the entire Kurt story, promising to explain everything to me so that I wouldn't have any lingering questions or confusion. I was so game and told them everything, and they broke it all down piece by piece. (I detailed the entire conversation in the introduction to my first book, *He's Not That Complicated*.) At the end I felt enlightened, clearheaded, and invigorated. Best of all, I felt empowered. Usually breakups left me feeling broken and empty and doubting myself. I always blamed myself when things fell apart, thinking I'd messed it all up and everything was my fault.

But now I knew the truth, now I knew what went on in Guy World when it came to relationships (and I did also discover some critical mistakes I had made along the way). So that's where the secrets to understanding men live, in the men themselves! And this is what the women of the world need, they need this information. If I'd had it before I could have saved myself years of heartache! After that night, I moved on from Kurt and never looked back.

But Eric was another story. <u>Now that I wasn't distracted anymore, thoughts of him crept back in,</u> I couldn't let it go. I needed to know what had gone wrong. <u>I knew he wasn't right for me, I knew I deserved better, I knew I was much better off out of the relationship than I'd ever been in it, but I still couldn't let it go.</u>

By now two years had gone by. He and Amy had broken up, and we hadn't had any contact save for a few texts I'd received from him the year before, which I'd received while out at some NYC hot spot having the time of my life and responded to with a few cold replies. I thought I'd hear more from him, but that hadn't come to pass.

Then one night I made a decision. I was going to call him. I needed to move on with my life and I couldn't do that without exorcising his ghost. We ended up talking until the sun came up, and he explained everything. Finally, I got my answers! They were more than anything I could have asked for, and the next day I woke up feeling as though literal shackles had been removed; I was finally free.

I thought that would be the end of it, but suddenly Eric was back in my life. At that point I was working as a fashion and beauty editor for a popular website, but I was itching to start my own thing. I had seen other girls do it and find success and I figured it couldn't be that hard...the only problem was I had minimal technical capabilities and didn't know where to begin. Eric is the opposite, something of a genius when it comes to technology, and before I knew it we were starting a website together and A New Mode (anewmode.com) was born.

Eric would run the business side and I would create the editorial content, with the exception of one feature that I couldn't write myself. I asked Eric to write a weekly "Ask a Guy" column, to give girls the clarity and knowledge I had gained both from him and from my relationship with Kurt. Eric had a strong background working as a dating coach and writing about relationships (he had also majored in Psychology like me) so I knew he would be perfect for the job. And he was! Before long, his "Ask a Guy" columns became a sensation, and we were getting flooded with questions from women around the world desperate to understand men's behavior.

In the beginning, I worked closely with Eric to make the section exactly what I'd envisioned it to be. I edited his content carefully and would push him in certain areas to go deeper, add more, really bring it home. The work paid off, and "Ask a Guy" was soon the number-one draw of the site, even though originally it was supposed to be mostly about fashion and beauty.

And I noticed a funny thing happening to me. Suddenly I got it, like really got it. I would be on dates with guys and just understand everything that was happening with perfect clarity. I was never left guessing how he felt or wondering if I would ever hear from him again. I just knew. Granted, in my own life I wasn't able to be as objective as I could be when it came to other people because my emotions occasionally clouded my judgment. But with my friends I became something of a superhero. They called my ability to read men my Spidey Sense and were awestruck by how dead-on I could be about relationships. I could predict exactly what would go down and how: if a guy was going to bail, if he was serious, if he was a keeper or a closet loser, if he would text back. (Not only that, I could even tell them when and what he would say!) My new superpower gave me a super dose of confidence, and I decided to write about relationships on ANM as well. I was nervous at first, worried that no one would take me seriously given I was a young single girl who had yet to find lasting love, but I received a very warm reception; our readers were able to relate to me and the struggles I had faced.

Before we go on, I'll answer some burning questions you probably have. Was it hard working with an ex at first? Yes. Was it awkward? Sometimes. Did old feelings re-emerge? Yes. Did we ever get back together? No. These are the questions I field regularly, and yes, while there were some rocky points and while it took a while to navigate the pain of the past, we got through it. We've been broken up for over ten years now, and I don't think either one of us is the same person we once were. It feels like a lifetime has passed. So is it weird working with an ex? I suppose it would be, but he doesn't even feel like an ex anymore.

So Who Am I and Why Should You Listen to Me?

Aside from majoring in psychology, I am not a formally trained relationship expert. All I have are my insights and experiences and ten years of giving relationship advice (and being told I'm pretty good at it!) I am also happily married to the cutest, sweetest, most amazing man I have ever known.

I have always believed that everything happens for a reason. Call me a doe-eyed optimist, but that is one of my convictions that has never really wavered. When I was 17, I met a boy who made my heart beat a little differently from the rest. He just had a certain something that I was never able to find again. The relationship wasn't serious, but it was significant. I was crazy about him. And I just remember feeling OK whenever I talked to him. I just felt *right*, like this was how things were supposed to be. I can't quite explain it; it was just this feeling of quiet calm. The relationship failed and he ended up being my first major heartbreak. I wanted something serious, he wanted to be a freshman in college and take nothing, save for an intense game of beer pong, seriously. I was crushed. I analyzed and replayed the relationship on loop for months. That was probably the start of my quest to understand men…the never-ending quest that turned into a career!

After our breakup a lot of stuff happened: college, Eric, my career, life. Every few years, he and I would fortuitously cross paths, and every time we did I felt that familiar flutter, that heady sensation. But nothing ever came of it…until something did. During one of our fortuitous meetings a magical thing happened, almost as though the stars had aligned. (It only took 11 years!) He and I were both single, both living in New York City, much more mature, and on the same page in so many ways. We started dating, got engaged, and now we're married!

Experience is the greatest teacher, and my relationship experiences have given me a wealth of invaluable knowledge.

My entire life has been consumed by relationships. Obviously I'm *in* a relationship, but I also spend most of my time reading about relationships (both books and research papers), talking to people about their relationships, writing about relationships, and observing relationships. It's a fascinating topic that I'll never get bored with because there is always so much more to learn. And that's the sad part, actually. It's such an important topic, but so few people get the education they need to have successful, happy relationships.

That's why I created A New Mode. I wanted to create a go-to resource that would be an ultimate guide to understanding relationships. All I really remember about that dark period of my life after Eric left me was feeling not good enough and alone. I felt so, so lonely. I felt like the pain was mine and mine alone, like no one could possibly understand. I remember becoming obsessed with the Brad Pitt-Jennifer Aniston-Angelina Jolie love triangle (I was obviously on Team Aniston) and rooting for Jen like she was my sister because I needed to see her happy, I needed to see that there is a light at the end of the tunnel, that being cheated on and left for someone else could still somehow result in a happy ending, that it would all be OK. I would look online, I would read books, I would even look for movies with plot lines that mirrored my life, but I never found the comfort I really needed.

Rejection can be a crushing, gutting experience, and even though there is much greater pain in the world, and even though I certainly am not the only girl to have had her heart broken, it truly felt like no one on the entire planet could possibly fathom what I was going through.

With A New Mode, I really aimed to create a place that

would foster that feeling of sisterhood, a place where women could find understanding and answers. I am still stunned by the fact that women, literally of all ages and from every corner of the world, write to us with the exact same questions, the exact same pain, and all they want are answers and understanding.

Had the situations I described not gone down exactly as they did, I wouldn't be able to write about relationships the way I do. I wouldn't have an arsenal of crazy dates and relationships gone bad to write about and use as examples. (Usually of what not to do!) I wouldn't be as strong and capable as I am. I wouldn't have been set on the path towards self-improvement that ultimately led me back to my first (and last) love.

You can't panic in the middle of the sentence. I panicked; I didn't think it would be OK. And it is so, so OK. Everything is better than I ever envisioned it could be. My experiences gave me depth and a refined worldview and made me more compassionate and able to speak to the pain of others. As for Eric, well I guess I always knew deep down he would be a significant person in my life, and he is. He helped me create this awesome community where I'm able to reach so many women; I'd say all that pain was worth it in the end!

Everything You Need to Know

I have written a lot over the years, like a lot. I have so much material in the form of articles, newsletters, books, and audio programs it literally took me two months to sort through it all (and I probably only got through half!) This book is a compilation of some of my best work. The content that hit the hardest, made the strongest impression, and really got people thinking and talking.

While my last book, *10 Things Every Woman Needs to Know About Men*, was all about understanding men and why they act the way they do (those questions really are where it all began) I wanted to create a resource that focused more on the experience of being in a relationship. This book applies whether you're single or spoken for, and I speak to both sides in equal measure. One key thing I've observed is that it takes the same skills to get a relationship as it does to be in a relationship—at least a happy, loving, mutually fulfilling relationship.

There are also plenty of new insights, stories, and ideas. I really wanted to look at why so many relationships falter and what it takes to avoid that and get the amazing relationship you've always wanted, but didn't know if it really existed or how to get it.

I organized this book in a way to really break it all down and make it crystal clear so you have no more questions, only clarity.

So let's dive in and look at exactly what you need to know to have the love you've always wanted.

1

Choosing the Right Guy

*Women cannot complain about men anymore
until they start getting better taste in them.*

– Bill Maher

All the relationship advice in the world won't make any difference if you're choosing the wrong guy. This is the step that often gets missed or overlooked. Women hammer away, trying to pound the proverbial square peg into a round hole, then wonder what they're doing wrong, why they can't seem to make it fit, why they can't get the love they want. You can't turn a losing stock into a winning stock. You can't force someone to change and to want what you want. You can't convince someone to feel a certain way about you.

I spent way too long chasing after guys who wouldn't or couldn't give me what I wanted, and then I wondered what was wrong with me when it didn't get me lasting love! The problem was simple: I was choosing the wrong men. It sounds straightforward enough, but it's a very tricky thing. We fall for these guys because it feels so right, because we're swept up in the passion, the chemistry, and the intoxicating aura of unavailability; we get sucked into the space that exists when someone is just beyond our reach and it makes us yearn for him. We convince ourselves that this is it, that he's the one and we just need to make him see it.

This is where the problems develop. This is where all the questions and tears and doubt and uncertainties and fears start to consume you. You mistake these feelings for true love because maybe you've never felt this way before, and you think it must be because this guy is different and this relationship is meant to last.

This is just a glimpse into the confusion that ensues when you choose the wrong guy. If you're hung up on a man who can't commit or won't commit or who is mean to you or who is just a mean person in general, a guy with baggage, a guy with serious issues, a guy who you think would be perfect "if only" he changed such and such, then you're setting yourself up to lose before you even begin, and you are blocking yourself from ever finding the love you want.

Where Healthy Relationships Begin

Before we talk about what to look for in a guy, it's important to look at how relationships begin. The start of a relationship can oftentimes color our lenses and sometimes lead us down a bad path and into a toxic relationship.

Here's a situation that may sound familiar to you (it was certainly a recurring theme for me in my single life!) You meet someone, something clicks, and suddenly it feels like a force outside of you has taken over.

After this encounter you can't—for the life of you—get this

guy out of your head. You try to think about other things but nothing works. You ruminate over every detail of your interaction with him—what he said, what you said, what his body language said. You think about the things you *wish* you had said.

You check your phone constantly to see if he called or texted. If he does, your stomach drops, your heart races, you want to leap off your seat and shout for joy. And then of course you need to figure out the exact right thing to say back to him, the perfect quip to show him that you're perfect for each other.

The high continues as you venture into a relationship, and it becomes even more intense. You never quite know where you stand with him. The uncertainty keeps you on your toes, constantly on alert for something that looks like a bad sign or an ominous foreshadowing. This emotional rollercoaster is as thrilling as it is exhausting. You're hooked. The worst possible thing that could happen is him leaving. It's a fear you can't quite shake no matter how promising the situation looks, a fear that drives everything you say and do.

Now another scenario.

You meet a guy, you think he's nice and all, you have a good conversation, and he gets your number. While you're pleased, you don't go into a tizzy over it. You may check his Facebook profile, but only for a few minutes. You are happy to hear from him if he calls or texts, but you don't notice the hours that pass in between your interactions. You go out a few times, not expecting much, but soon enough your interest and attraction begin to grow. Things feel calm, there's no drama, no heart palpitations … and it feels really nice.

Which relationship do you think has a stronger chance of survival?

Instinctively, you would say the second one. In real life, you would fall for the first. That's because the first scenario illustrates everything we've ever been told about love.

In movies and romance novels, love is this grand, all-consuming force that takes you over in the most dramatic of ways. There are huge obstacles to overcome, but it's OK because love conquers all! I mean, would any of us have cared for "The Notebook" if Ali and Noah were of the same social status, went on a few lukewarm dates, then got to know each other and developed a deepening connection over time? Don't think so.

Unhealthy Relationships Start with a Pull

Relationships that start from a place of pure, unadulterated passion can seldom survive unless they have some substance and depth of connection to stand on. Explosive chemistry isn't what creates a lasting, healthy relationship. It can lead to great sex and feelings of euphoria, and you may come to understand why they say love is a drug, but no matter how intense and all consuming, that sort of thing is seldom sustainable long term.

When you feel a strong and sudden pull towards someone else, the kind that causes you to turn him from mere mortal to deity-like being, something sinister is usually at play. OK, maybe not sinister, but something that isn't exactly what you would term romantic. There are a few good reasons why we might become inexplicably drawn to someone who isn't good for us.

Imago Theory

This theory, developed by clinical pastoral counselor Harville Hendrix, Ph.D., posits that the pull we feel towards another person is guided by our unconscious desire to rectify some issue from our past. Imago is Latin for image, and the theory essentially states that we unconsciously seek partners who reflect the image of our primary caregivers so that we can try to heal lingering wounds inflicted by them by working through issues with someone in their image. These relationships present the opportunity to heal ourselves and become whole again, but they also pose the risk of continuing to pour salt into open wounds.

How it pans out is something like this: if your parents always made you feel like you weren't good enough, you may seek out guys who make you feel like you're not good enough, then try to win them over in an attempt to rectify those painful feelings from your past.

*If your father was very critical, you may find yourself drawn to a man who is very critical, trying to win his love and approval in order to heal from the hurt of your father's rejection. These decisions aren't conscious, they happen very deep beneath the surface in areas we can't easily access. When we meet someone, we immediately sense everything about him, especially the way he makes us feel (again, this happens unconsciously).

On a conscious level, you may assess the things he says, but on an unconscious level, you're looking at his body language, his tone, the way he phrases things, how much eye contact he makes, his whole demeanor. If your unconscious finds something familiar in that person, something that reminds you of an unresolved hurt from the past, it will light up and push you towards that person.*

You may also unconsciously seek out partners who have some quality that is underdeveloped in you. For example, if you're a Type A workaholic and always wished you could ease up, you may be drawn to a laid-back partner who isn't so driven.

Maybe this sounds a little too New Agey to you, or maybe it doesn't describe your situation at all, but it's a powerful concept and it has gained a lot of praise and recognition in the field of psychology so it's worth considering. I know I've seen some of this at play in my own dating life.

Infatuation

Being infatuated sounds like a grand, romantic thing, but it can actually be quite dangerous. The problem with infatuation is it isn't based on anything real. Infatuation causes you to fall in love with an image rather than an actual person. It causes you to put someone on a pedestal and overlook his flaws. Since he's so "perfect," you become afraid to be yourself—I mean, how could your true self *ever* compete with perfection?

You don't want to say the wrong thing and scare him off, so you aren't genuine in your interactions. You rely on his approval so desperately that you also become a bit needy. You may not act needy, but it's something that lurks beneath the surface and he will pick up on it … men always do. You lose your sense of worth because it becomes so wrapped up in how he feels about you.

Healthy Relationships Build Slowly

Healthy relationships usually begin with mutual interest and attraction that grows over time. This is the complete opposite of unhealthy relationships, which usually start out with a grand light show that quickly simmers into ash. If you can internalize this, it will change the way you date forever.

The most important trait to develop is objectivity. No one really talks about that because it's not so sexy, but if you want to find lasting love and prevent yourself from getting hurt, you'll need to learn how to use your head a little more than your heart, at least in the beginning. Your heart can lead you into all kinds of bad places. Your heart is the one that tells you it's a great idea to go for the bad boy who's just so dreamy, even when he's out on parole and struggling with addictions, or has told you he won't be in a committed relationship, ever. Your heart convinces you that the heart wants what the heart wants and who are you to deny your heart? Your heart doesn't operate according to reason or rational. It makes you do things that you later look back on and wonder, what was I thinking? But you weren't thinking, that's not what the heart does. OK, I know I'm being mean to the heart. It does have its benefits, but that comes later. In the beginning of a relationship, it's best to remain as objective as possible and try to keep your emotions mostly contained.

The best way to do this is to try to go slowly. Ease into the relationship instead of diving in head first. This will create an environment for you to allow your level of interest and attraction to grow steadily over time, rather than flooding you all at once in a big emotional tsunami.

If you spend all your time with him, you risk overlooking critical information about who he really is and if the relationship is built to last. Just because two people feel strongly for each other it doesn't always mean they can be together.

It is imperative to have a foundation of compatibility, shared goals and interests, and common values. Some things simply can't be negotiated. Before you emotionally invest, it is wise to determine if you are *fundamentally compatible*. And the best way to do this is to go slowly. I don't necessarily mean physically, I mean emotionally.

When you first meet someone, you want to spend every minute of every day with him. You talk for hours and hours on the phone, text all day, you can't get enough. The obvious reason this is problematic is because you may end up relying too heavily on the relationship for your happiness, but also, you don't get a break from the emotional excitement and stimulation of it all. Then, if you realize this guy may not be right for you, you'll be in too deep to get yourself out of the situation. You'll instead rely on some cliché like "love conquers all" to justify staying with him.

I am not saying to stay away from guys you feel a strong immediate attraction to and only date guys you're only "meh" about. I think you should date both kinds of guy—the infatuation guy could turn out to be a loser and the "meh" guy could turn out to be the love of your life. (I've seen it happen countless times!)

Either way you have to date smart. This will come more

naturally with "meh" than it will with the object of your infatuation.

If you just met or just started seeing someone, I strongly advise that you try to limit how much time you spend with him early on. Try to not go on more than two dates a week or engage in marathon texting sessions that go all day. When you do this, you never get a break from the emotional high and you don't get a chance to come back down and recalibrate.

So many girls make the mistake of getting caught up in how the guy feels about them rather than focusing on how they feel about him.

You can avoid falling into this trap by doing regular reality checks. Make sure you see him and the situation clearly. The best way to do this is to make sure you can recognize his flaws. The way you know you're infatuated is if you see no flaws. *Everyone* has flaws.

Why it Matters

When you get in over your head, you may convince yourself that something like him wanting to live only in the country and you wanting to live only in the city is not such a big deal. Someone who maintains a more objective perspective would acknowledge that she would be miserable living in the country, and since this guy wouldn't choose to live anywhere else, she would get out of the situation.

I've seen (and personally experienced) many situations where a couple breaks up after a long period of time because of some issue that was apparent right from the beginning—they're different religions, want to live in different states, one person doesn't want kids.

In every one of these situations, the couple believed that things would magically just work out. Imagine how much time and effort they would have saved and heartbreak they would have avoided had they been dating with their heads instead of their hearts from the beginning.

Qualities That Make Him a Keeper

A lot of women write to me begging to understand why their relationships always fail…why guys treat them badly…why they always get hurt…why they can't get a guy to commit. The common thread in most of these cases is that these women are choosing men who clearly are not husband—or even relationship—material and hoping that by some chance the men will suddenly transform into the knights in shining armor they want. This type of situation doesn't exist anywhere aside from cheesy romantic comedies. If you choose to pursue a relationship with a guy who clearly isn't relationship material, then you're setting yourself up to fail before you even begin.

Trust me, I know all too well how enticing those damage cases can be. Sure, he has emotional issues, he's jaded, he's struggling at work, he has no direction, he still acts like a frat boy even though his acting-like-a-drunk-idiot-and-getting-away-with-it days expired years ago, but there's a really great guy underneath all that and as soon as we deal with all this other stuff, *then* we'll have an amazing relationship. I'm sorry, but no.

The problem with these damage cases is that they often have a lot of the qualities we want, but not the ones we actually *need*. There is a big difference between wants and needs when it comes to relationships, but it's not always easy to make the distinction. You might want a guy who is tall and strapping and charismatic and a CEO of a major company, but a guy with those credentials might have a host of other qualities that aren't good for you and don't fulfill your fundamental emotional needs. My husband is the opposite of the "ideal man" I had envisioned for myself, but even though he doesn't have certain qualities I used to consider requirements, he is exactly what I need. That was clear to me and everyone around me very early into our relationship.

When I hit that stage in life where I realized I was done dating for the sake of dating and wanted to settle down and find "the one," I realized that the kinds of guys I liked to date weren't necessarily husband material, and I had to really examine my list of wants and needs and figure out the differences between the two. Doing so made all the difference. Suddenly the damage cases who were once *oh so appealing* did nothing for me.

Whether you're single, dating, or in a serious relationship, these are the most essential qualities you need to look for in a man, the ones that tell you beyond a shadow of a doubt that he's the one and this is it.

- **He loves your good qualities and accepts and embraces the bad without making you feel guilty for having flaws.** You don't need to hide your true self from him and put on a front in order to be what you think he wants. You can share your true self and be vulnerable and feel safe doing so, knowing that if anything it will make him feel even closer to you.

- **He is there for you when you need him, even if it's inconvenient for him.** A partnership will sometimes require sacrifice and compromise. Life is unpredictable and unexpected. You can't predict what will happen and nothing can possibly go as planned 100% of the time. A guy who is husband material will be there for you when you need him. He will be in it with you; he will be your partner in whatever happens and will weather the storm with you, even though he might prefer to stay in the sunshine.

- **He considers you when making decisions, both big and small.** A relationship is a partnership, not a dictatorship. Factoring you in shows that he respects you and that he wants to create a life with you, not simply envelope you in his world. Our worlds can be comfortable when we don't have to compromise, so it's not always easy taking someone else into account and factoring in their wants and needs and preferences, but that's what a relationship is.

- **He is growth oriented.** No one is perfect; we all have flaws. And these flaws aren't black and white—usually a person's greatest strength is linked to his greatest weakness. In a relationship, his behavior affects you (and vice versa) and sometimes his less developed traits will have a negative impact on you. A growth-oriented guy will want to work to strengthen his character. A guy who isn't growth oriented will say it's your problem and that this is just the way he is and you need to deal with it. For example, let's say you're dating a guy who can be insensitive at times. Maybe he doesn't give you emotional support when you've had a rough day and instead just gives you matter of fact advice in a direct way. His no-nonsense approach to solving problems might be useful to him in the workplace, but it might be hurtful to you sometimes when he doesn't empathize with what you're going through and instead just tells you what to do about it, or gets impatient by the fact that you're upset over something he doesn't consider to be that big of a deal. You want a guy who will accept that his tone can come across as harsh and hurtful to you and who actually tries to work on it, not one who says it's your problem and you need to deal with it. He probably won't get it right every time, but if he's growth oriented he will at least try.

- **He has similar beliefs and values.** This one seems so obvious yet it's so often overlooked. Love does not in fact conquer all. If you are not fundamentally compatible, you will face major hurdles ahead. If he is going to be your life partner, you have to make sure you are both on the same page when it comes to issues that matter. And if you aren't on the same page, then make sure he respects where you stand (and vice versa) and that you're both willing to work together to reach a mutually fulfilling understanding about your differences. Everyone's values are different. For some, their values will be rooted in religion. Other people value a strong work ethic, while some value a commitment to a healthy lifestyle. It may sound trivial, but I've seen very serious, long-term relationships end because one person couldn't deal with the other's lack of ambition or motivation.

- **He views you as his partner.** The relationship is something more than each of you individually…together, you and he are a team. And as that team, you are both individually stronger than you could be on your own. He sees you as his equal, as a person of great value, someone he can grow with. Not someone who is there to feed his ego, give him validation, be his emotional crutch, or be there solely to satisfy his needs. He respects everything about you—your thoughts, ambitions, opinions, the things you say, the company you keep, your job. He doesn't make you feel bad about your life circumstances and he appreciates the person you are and the choices you have made.

- **He wants to make you happy.** One of a man's most fundamental needs in a relationship is to make his girl happy. It may not always feel like it or look like it, but it's true. In order to truly bond with a woman, a man needs to feel like he can make her happy. And when a man truly cares for a woman, he wants to do whatever it takes to make her happy. Love is a selfless thing. If you love people because they make you feel great about yourself, then it isn't real love. When a man shows he genuinely cares about you and your happiness, even if it sometimes comes at the expense of his own happiness, then you know his feelings are for real.

- **He communicates with you, even about tough issues and even if one of you is upset with the other.** With the right guy, you won't be afraid of bringing up certain things for fear of rocking the boat. You know he respects you and will see what you have to say as valid and important. Every relationship will face its share of obstacles. There will be fights, miscommunications, arguments, and also times when one partner isn't feeling loved. The only way to emerge from the tough times better and stronger is to work through them together, and this starts with open communication.

- **He wants the same kind of commitment you want.** A guy can have all the qualities on this list, but if he doesn't want to marry you (or commit in the way you want), or maybe doesn't want to get married in general, then he is not for you. When a guy is ready to get married and meets a girl he thinks he can spend his life with, he knows pretty early on. That's not to say he'll get engaged right away, but he knows this is it and she knows it too. Maybe he tells her or maybe it's so obvious he doesn't even need to. It might be the wrong time, maybe he wants to wait until he's more established in his career or more financially stable, but he will still convey his level of commitment; she won't be left hanging and guessing and wondering. If he still feels like he has wild oats to sow and is drawn to the single, bachelor, party-boy lifestyle, he is not commitment minded and you are setting yourself up for disappointment. If what you want is a serious, lasting commitment, make sure he is on the same page before you become invested. When a guy is ready for a serious commitment, it's usually pretty obvious. And if it isn't, then bring it up and discuss it with him. If he's husband material, he'll understand. If he isn't…then at least now you know before it's too late! And yes, I understand that not every woman makes getting married a goal and I respect that. But I'm speaking to those who want a lasting commitment, be it marriage or a partnership without a legal piece of paper.

But the Most Important Quality of All is…

He wants to make it work. He's willing to put in any amount of effort. If there is a problem, he wants to find a way to solve it. He wants to work harder, to be better, to be his best self. The important thing to keep in mind is that people have different ideas about what it means to put effort into a relationship. He might believe that working hard and being good at his job is putting in effort because he wants to provide for you and give you nice things and a comfortable lifestyle. (I use this as an example because it's a classic point of contention between men and women: she will often view him working too much as him putting no effort into the relationship and being married to his work).

I remember the exact moment I knew my husband was the one. After about a month of everything being perfect (as they usually are in the beginning), we had our first conflict. It was nothing major; we just started experiencing areas where our personalities clashed and seeing how we process things differently. I tend to be more intellectual and straightforward in my thinking, while he's more emotional and dynamic in his thinking. I would get impatient with this, and my impatience was hurtful to him. The details don't really matter, what matters is that I remember the way he brought the issue up and how sincere he was about working through things and getting to a place of better understanding.

I have seen countless variations of this kind of scenario: girl is dating a guy, things are going great (again, as they often do in the beginning), but then they hit that inevitable point of conflict. Maybe she acts needy or maybe he gets distant, but whatever happens suddenly things aren't as seamless as they were the week before. Then he decides he can't hang anymore and tells her he "doesn't have time for a relationship" or he can't give her what she needs. The girl racks her brain trying to figure out what she did wrong, what she could have done differently.

She thinks if she hadn't been so needy, if she had been a little more chilled out, if she hadn't done this and instead done that. Really, the only way things would have turned out differently is if she had behaved perfectly according to his script, if she'd never disagreed or been unhappy with him, if she'd been perfectly in alignment with his thoughts and what he wanted in a partner. That sounds reasonable, right? (That's sarcasm in case it didn't come across!)

If a guy leaves when things get a little rocky, it means he is lacking in the most important quality you need in a partner, and that is a man who is committed not only to you, but to making it work. It's easy to be in a relationship when everything is all sunshine and roses. The truth comes out after time goes on, when you let your guard down, when you can be more of yourselves instead of the absolute best version of yourselves. Even the best couples don't seamlessly fit together. There is always a certain degree of work involved in order to create that deep and meaningful connection, and it has to come from both people.

When a guy is ready to settle down and sees you as a good potential partner, he wants to make it work. He wants to overcome the differences, to get to a place of better understanding. My husband and I are so different. The way we think and feel is different, and the way we communicate is different. In the beginning of our relationship this definitely caused problems, but now, after really committing to working on it, we have hit this amazing place of understanding and are so much more in sync. The differences still exist, but we were able to meet in the middle. Even when things got difficult, I wasn't any less sure he was the guy for me because of how deeply committed he was to making it work.

A big mistake I see women making is blaming themselves when a relationship falls apart. They torture themselves with could haves and should haves. I should have been less needy, I should have been more agreeable, I could have been more supportive, etc. Yeah, you could have done all that, but it wouldn't have mattered if he wasn't committed to making it work.

There will always be differences, there will always be problems, you will not always behave exactly how he wants a partner to behave (same for him).

A relationship isn't about finding the perfect match, it's about finding someone you can form a meaningful, lasting partnership with. Notice the word *form*. It's an active process; it doesn't just exist. It's about working together, being a team, and overcoming the challenges.

Some people have deal-breakers and that's that. Maybe it's religion or where to live or lifestyle preferences. But all the other stuff—personality quirks, your nature, your ways of interacting in social settings, your fundamental traits…either he's in it or he's not. And if he's not, then there is nothing you can do.

Red Flags You Should Never Ignore

Every relationship is different and comes with a unique set of circumstances. However, there are some universal standards that indicate a guy isn't the right one for you, a few red flags that should never be ignored but usually are.

You Don't Trust Him

Without trust, there is no relationship. Period. In a good, strong, healthy relationship you feel at ease. You feel safe. You feel secure. You do not feel constantly panicked and on edge, always anticipating the proverbial other shoe to drop.

If you don't believe the things he tells you or are always questioning his motives and his whereabouts, there is something majorly amiss. You can't spend your life constantly on the lookout; that's just exhausting.

Sometimes a lack of trust develops because of something substantial. Maybe he cheated, maybe you caught him in a few too many lies. And sometimes it's something that lingers in the pit of your gut. Even though you can't quantify the reason, you just don't feel like you can trust this person. Either way, it's a big red flag and a major sign that your relationship isn't going to last.

If he cheated on you or lied to you, then you'll have to be honest with yourself when you decide if you can truly move past it and if you really, genuinely believe that he'll never do the same thing again. If you can't get to that place, then there isn't much point in sticking it out. You're just setting yourself up for a life in which you always feel paranoid and insecure. Relationships are supposed to bring out your best, not your worst.

If you can't quite pinpoint the reason for your trust issues, you should listen to your gut. Our gut instincts can be incredibly powerful. Just make sure you aren't projecting your own insecurities onto him and aren't making him pay for the sins of a cheating/lying ex.

There Is No Depth of Connection

Sexual chemistry is great and is definitely important, but that alone can't sustain a relationship. An amazing sex life is only one piece of the puzzle, yet for a lot of couples it's the only leg the relationship has to stand on. I know so, so many women who got so engulfed by the intoxicating chemistry they experienced with their partner that they overlooked every sign that clearly showed he wasn't the one...and wasn't even that great of a person.

For a relationship to last, you need to have depth of connection. You need to know your partner intimately, and this goes way beyond his bedroom skills. You need to know who he is, what he wants out of life, and what his hopes, dreams, and fears are. You need to connect to each other in an honest, unguarded way.

Each person is composed of many layers. In our lives, some people see the surface layer, a select few see what lies beneath the exterior, and very few see straight to the core. Your life partner should be in the last group.

Knowing the basics about someone isn't knowing who they are. If you know the same things about your guy as most of the other people in his life, then you don't have much depth of connection.

Fortunately, this issue is one that can be fixed. Try to make an effort to connect to him in a real way. If he resists, or you still don't feel like you're connecting in a significant way, then it means he's probably not that invested in you or the relationship. Or maybe you're just not the right fit for one another.

Attraction and sexual chemistry are never enough to sustain a relationship. If that's all you have that's fine, but you might want to move on if you're serious about finding the one.

Lack of Respect

Respect is the most overlooked element when it comes to making a relationship work, but it's one of the most essential. If you're going to have a long-lasting, healthy relationship, you must respect your partner and he must respect you.

Respect is huge for guys. In fact, I'd say it's the number one thing men want out of their relationship. Just as most women need to feel loved and adored, men need to feel respected and admired. A man needs to feel like the man; he needs to feel respected. If you don't respect him or the way he lives his life, he will resent you and will not want to be with you long term.

At the same time, you need to be with a partner who respects you. This means he respects you as a person: your beliefs, your aspiration, and especially your boundaries.

Eye rolling has actually been shown by famous relationship researcher John Gottman to be a big predictor of divorce, and it's no surprise…eye rolling is a manifestation of contempt, which is the opposite of respect.

He Brings Out Your Worst

As I mentioned earlier, relationships are supposed to bring out your best. The sad fact is, a lot of women end up shackled to a person who brings out their worst.

Sometimes you might not even recognize the person that your relationship has turned you into. That was definitely the case for me many years back before I knew any better. I made the same mistake countless women make. I got so caught up in my feelings for the guy that I overlooked the fact that I didn't really like myself all that much when I was around him.

Throughout the course of my yearlong relationship with Eric, I was unrecognizable from my previous confident, happy, positive self. Instead I felt insecure, panicked, anxious, and perpetually on edge, but I couldn't let go because of my strong feelings for him. Those feelings locked me in a tight grip, and it was only when the relationship inevitably imploded that I was able to see just how toxic the situation truly was.

It wasn't that he was a bad guy; he was just bad for me. It's a fact that would have saved me years of heartache had I realized it sooner. While getting myself out of that relationship felt impossible, the end was always inevitable because we brought out the worst in each other.

The point is, a relationship should lift you higher, not drag you down. It should help you reach your potential and become the best version of yourself. Of course relationships can't be all sunshine and roses all the time. They take patience and work. But this work leads to a positive place, a place of growth and understanding and more love and connection. Bad relationships are ones where the work involved is expending energy on fighting and arguing and trying to win. A relationship won't always feel perfect and pleasant, but overall it will help you grow into a better person, as long as you're with a good guy who is committed to making it work and loves and appreciates you for who you are.

He Doesn't Take Responsibility

One of the biggest relationship red flags is when someone won't take responsibility for anything and instead blames you, maybe using a justification along the lines of, "Well I wouldn't yell at you if you weren't being so annoying." Rather than admitting when he's wrong, he comes up with excuses and justifications for his behaviors and reasons to blame you.

One of the biggest indicators of psychopaths or sociopaths is not being able to take responsibility; it's a fundamental lack of empathy that prevents them from ever being able to see the other person's perspective. However, it doesn't always start out this way. In the beginning he's enraptured by you and everything you do is right. Then suddenly he's unhappy and he blames you for everything that's wrong. If you erroneously reason that you're the problem, he may feed this mentality. You don't inspire him enough, you don't give him what he needs, you aren't supportive enough, you're always negative. It's always you, never him.

I'm not saying every guy who can't take responsibility is a psycho; he could just be immature. But it is something to keep in mind because narcissists are out there and this is one of their key features.

He's Selfish

I have a friend who was seeing a guy she really liked, and she continued to date him even though he was clearly a bit immature and selfish and not ready to settle down (we joked that he had her "sexmotized" and that's why she wasn't able to break free of his spell). There were signs of trouble all over the place, but most were little things and that's why they were easy to sweep under the rug.

For example, one night she suggested they go to a vegetarian Indian restaurant she loved, and he got all pissy and said there wasn't a point in going out for Indian food if he couldn't eat meat. Never mind the fact that he always chose the restaurants, that they always did what he wanted, that they always slept at his apartment because that's what he wanted, or the fact that he had told her to pick a place for dinner. It was the one time she got to decide something, and she was overruled because it wasn't what he wanted.

This may seem like a silly example, but it demonstrates the essence of selfishness, one that will continue to pop up when dealing with a selfish person. And in that relationship, it did, over and over until finally she couldn't take it anymore and ended it. (This launched the make-up and break-up cycle for a while, because that's what happens when you linger in a relationship with the wrong guy, but eventually they cut it off for good.)

Selfish people also tend to engage in selfish love. That is, they love you when you make them feel good; when you're behaving how they want you to, they're the best partners ever.

41

When you go off script, then they withdraw and won't do anything for you in a sort of tit-for-tat retaliation.

That's not how a relationship works. A relationship isn't there to serve one person. It's a partnership and it's about working together, not one person working for the other.

Let Your Gut Be Your Guide

I mentioned the importance of listening to your gut earlier and want to get into it a little deeper because it's an essential skill, one that can keep you out of sticky situations.

At the end of the day, you usually already know the answers to your dating questions. The lists I provided of qualities to look for and red flags to watch out for can help you see things more clearly, maybe making it harder to hide from what's right in front of you, but oftentimes you already know. You know when a guy isn't worthy of you—when you're wasting your time, when you're not being treated the way you would like to be treated or the way you know you deserve to be treated—but you push this knowledge down because you just don't want to deal with it. You don't want to deal with a breakup, with putting yourself back on the market, with dating more guys, navigating the waters, trying to find a guy who cares about you. You don't want to because it's exhausting! It seems somehow easier to stick with what's broken and try to just make it work.

In a good, strong, healthy relationship, you feel loved and secure. You don't question whether your man is using you and if the things he says are genuine. You just feel at ease. Feeling constantly on edge, waiting anxiously for the other shoe to drop, is usually a sign that something is amiss and your instincts are trying to open your eyes to a reality you don't want to see.

Your gut is a powerful tool in relationships. It's something we all possess and it can be fine-tuned to work optimally. The way to get in touch with it is to listen to what it's telling you. Listen to that small, quiet voice that gently tells you: "You deserve more than this, you don't need this guy."

The voice of your ego is loud and overpowering. It tells you "Of course he's the guy for you! So what if he disappears for days at a time, he told you that you were the most amazing women he's ever met, so I mean, DUH! He loves you."

Your ego shouts over the noise and convinces you that the outcome you want is reality because it has a lot at stake should this not be the case.

Most people allow their egos to get so entangled in their relationships that when the relationship collapses, their ego comes crashing down with it and then absolute misery ensues.

Our unconscious mind has a whole arsenal of information that our conscious
mind doesn't have easy access to. It has stored up pretty much everything that's ever happened to us and makes decisions accordingly.

Have you ever met someone and liked him right away even though you barely knew him? Or maybe you meet someone who seems perfectly nice, but you just can't stand her? This is the unconscious at work. The people we're drawn to often-times remind us of people we've had positive encounters with in the past. So too with the people we don't like right off the bat.

You can pick up on things subconsciously without even realizing it, and it will cause you to have a feeling that you can't quite pinpoint or explain.

The point is, most of the time you already know the answer. The problem is that you wish it were a different answer so instead of accepting it you whittle away what you know with rationalizations.

Here are a few tips to help you get better acquainted with your gut:

- **Ask yourself a question and listen for the immediate answer.** For example, if you're debating whether or not to dump your boyfriend, ask yourself: "Should I break up with him?" and listen to what first pops into your head. The real answer will most often come first, and then the excuses and justifications will pile on top.

- **Make the decision and then listen to your body.** If it's a bad decision you'll feel an aversion to it, usually in the pit of your stomach.

- **Check with a friend.** It can help to get an outsider's perspective because sometimes we can mistake wishful thinking for our gut instincts. Talk to a friend you trust for a dose of objectivity.

- **Practice mindfulness.** Most people live their lives bouncing from one thing to the next—work, errands, happy hour. There isn't that much time to listen to our own thoughts. Try to stay mindful and conscious throughout the day and check in with yourself to see what you're thinking and feeling. It also helps to set aside some reflection time. You can use this time to meditate, do yoga, journal, take a walk around the park—anything that will give you the space to check in with yourself.

Remember This

Choice is everything. It will largely determine if a relationship succeeds and lasts or fails and leaves you broken-hearted. The good news is that you have the power to choose the man you let into your life. Choose wisely!

2

What Is Love, Anyway?

*We always believe our first love is our last, and
our last love our first.*

– George John Whyte-Melville

When I was younger, I couldn't *wait* to fall in love. I vividly
remember getting frozen yogurt with a group of girl friends
when we were in middle school and one of my friends saying,
"Guys, how excited are you to fall in love?" The rest of us
couldn't help but giggle at the silliness of her statement ... but
we all felt an undeniable rush of excitement over the prospect
and nodded in agreement.

I loved Eric with all my heart, with every fiber of my being
... and let me tell you, it was nothing like the movies. While
he loved me very much, there were too many other variables
that stood in our way, and the relationship was always strained
and on the brink of implosion. We had maybe a month of
being drunk on love ... and then almost a year of pain and
problems. I didn't understand; *this isn't how it's supposed to
be.* The challenges and differences aren't supposed to matter
... it's supposed to all just work itself out and then you make
promises of forever and you keep them, and of course a hap-

pily ever after is the expected and rightful reward for making it through the storm.

The last thing in the world I ever anticipated was for my one true love to so abruptly fall out of love with me ... and in love with someone else. It left me broken, jaded, and utterly confused. Was it not really love? It sure felt like it, but true love is supposed to last forever, isn't it?

The reason so many of us have a hard time recognizing real love and making a relationship last is because most of us don't get any formal education in these areas; instead, our beliefs and ideas about love come from the mainstream media ... not exactly the most reliable source! And even if we ignore all that, many of us learn faulty and unreliable ideas about love from our parents and families. We might eventually learn to recognize certain things as unhealthy or even dysfunctional, but that doesn't mean we have a clue what healthy and functional looks like!

So let's break it down and uncover the truth about love and relationships, the good and the bad.

Top Five Biggest Misconceptions about Love

I'd say just about every person on the planet is seeking, or trying to maintain, lasting love. The problem is most of us have longstanding, firmly ingrained, highly unrealistic ideas of what love is *supposed* to be, and feel frustrated when reality falls short.

No one would deny that love is a beautiful, transformative

experience, but at the same time, it's important to have a realistic understanding of what it actually is.

Here are some of the biggest myths about what love is:

1. It's Supposed to be Difficult

The predominant depiction of love in movies and on TV is that it's supposed to be a challenge, something you fight for at all costs and don't ever give up on. While this certainly makes for good entertainment, it's not a realistic portrayal of love.

Relationships do take work, but falling in love (in a healthy way) is a relatively effortless process. It's not filled with hours of analyzing what he meant when he said XYZ...or feeling a sense of impending doom at all times...or making grand sacrifices and compromising who you are for the sake of the one you love. Who can forget the final scene in "Grease" when Sandy ditches the poodle skirt and sweater set for second-skin black leggings, an edgy bomber jacket, and a cigarette between her lips while Danny literally falls at her feet, overcome by pure lust and a need to have her right there in the carnival fun-house.

This is *not* what love looks like! When someone truly loves you, you will not have to mold yourself in order to fit with him; the pieces will naturally click.

The drama so often associated with love usually only applies to unhealthy relationships, ones that result from infatuation, obsession, or unrealistic expectations, not a genuine connection. A healthy, loving relationship is one where two people can be their authentic selves and look at what they can give to the relationship, rather than what they can get from it.

Both people complement each other and are able to give what the other needs and happily receive what their partner has to give. You should never have to fight for someone's love, or plot ways to make someone love you. When it's real and genuine, it will flow easily and effortlessly.

2. Love Conquers All

From music to movies to literature, everywhere you turn in mainstream media you hear love is all you need, love conquers all, love lifts us up where we belong...I could go on and on. Love is for sure a beautiful thing. Love is also necessary in order for a relationship to last, but it's not enough. Sometimes two people just don't fit. It's unfortunate, but it's a fact.

The reason most people are so jaded is they stay in relationships that aren't working for way too long. They try to be what the other person needs, they try to make it work by any means necessary, they try with all their might and they wind up broken and defeated. You simply cannot shove a square peg into a round hole. It doesn't matter how many ways you try, you will never be able to make it fit.

There's this idea that if you love someone enough, it will just work out. But sometimes it doesn't. It doesn't mean your love wasn't real, it just means that there were other factors at play and as a result, it just couldn't work long term.

While love is very powerful and capable of conquering some things, it isn't always strong enough to conquer other things, like different backgrounds, values, goals, and visions for the future, for example. Most of all, love simply cannot conquer incompatibility.

3. Only True Love Lasts

An important truth to realize is that not all love is meant to last; sometimes it's just part of the journey. Loving someone does not mean they are the right person for you. It doesn't guarantee you a happily ever after. More often than love leading to marriage, love leads to heartbreak...but the heartbreak can lead to growth, and that growth can lead to another love, one that can lead to a lasting marriage.

I have loved several wrong people in my life. While some of those experiences left me with a lot of shattered pieces to put back together, time has shown that none of those guys were right for me. It doesn't mean the love we shared was flawed or not enough, it just means we weren't compatible.

The sad fact is that many relationships end with bitterness and hate. One or both people leave the relationship thinking they were owed something, and they blame the other for not following through on this unwritten promise. If we could all just realize that love does not guarantee a happy ending, we would be able to move forward much more easily and start a new relationship with an open heart, rather than one shrouded in pain and disappointment.

4. You "Just Know" When It's Right

One of the biggest misconceptions about love is that you "just know" when you find the "right one." This mentality frees you of all responsibility in your love life...you don't need to work on yourself or prepare for love, just go about your business and someday the right one will drop into your life and you'll just know.

In order to fall in love with the right person, you need to be in the right place emotionally. If you don't find love from within, you will never be able to let it in from the outside. No one likes to talk about this though because it takes work, and the idea of some perfect person just entering your life and being the other half of you, the yin to your yang, is just so much easier and far more romantic.

In order to correctly identify the right one for you, you need to know who you are. You need to know your values, your boundaries, your fundamental needs, your wants, what you can compromise on, and what your absolute deal-breakers are. When you are in this place and the right person comes along, the one who understands you and sees you and connects with you and can give you what you need in a relationship, it will feel right and you will just *know*…but only because you've prepared yourself for love and are in the right place emotionally.

It's also worth noting that love is something that can grow over time; there aren't always instant fireworks that erupt as soon as your eyes meet. Often women reject perfectly good guys after a few dates because they "just didn't feel it." I'm not saying you should settle, but I am saying you should adjust your idea of what love should feel like. I know plenty of happily married women who almost didn't give their now husbands a second date. I'm not saying love at first sight can't, or doesn't, ever happen—it does, I've seen it—but it doesn't guarantee you a happier, more fulfilling relationship. It's just another means to get to the same destination, one that can be just as easily achieved slowly. (Side note: what we call "love at first sight" is really intense lust and desire coupled with the recognition that there is the potential to create something meaningful with this other person. You can't possibly know someone well enough on the first date to actually love him, but you can recognize the potential to create love with him.)

Often we reject the guys who would be good to us (and for us) because we are not yet in a place where we can receive true love. Instead we feel drawn to the guys who are unavailable, and we get caught up in trying to prove our worth and show him we're good enough. This toxic dating style happens when you don't feel worthy of love on some level...and going after these kinds of guys validates that notion.

The funny thing about the human mind, whether you realize it or not, is it's always looking to validate beliefs, no matter how damaging those beliefs are. If you believe no one likes you, your mind will ignore all the evidence that you are likable and will hone in on only those specific incidents when someone rejected you.

A big part of preparing yourself for love is letting go of resentments from the past, whether they stem from problems with exboyfriends, your parents, or your friends. Make an effort to let go of any lingering resentment you feel, because the truth is that holding onto this negativity is hurting you more than anyone else. When you hold onto faulty beliefs such as, "All men are commitment phobes" or "The guys I like always dump me," you sow the seeds for self-fulfilling prophecies.

For example, when you carry the idea around that all men are afraid of commitment, you will instinctively put up walls and won't trust the guys you date. As a result, you will never be able to get to that level of openness and trust necessary to create the kind of connection that leads to love.

5. Love is All You Need

When we think of what it takes to have a lasting, happy relationship, we of course say love is the most essential ingredient. Next usually comes good communication, shared goals, and the like. But no one ever talks about the importance of lust.

Love and lust are often painted as opposites, with the former being pure, transcendent, and full of light while the latter is depraved and full of darkness. They say love is giving, lust is taking; love is selfless, lust is selfish. While in its pure, isolated state lust can be a negative thing, so can love (at least, in romantic relationships). When your relationship is pure love, you have a level of comfort and familiarity.

Married people and couples who live together know what this is like. You love your partner very much, and can be completely comfortable around him...but sometimes things become a little *too* comfortable and the passion you once felt is nowhere to be found. This isn't the result of lack of love; it's lack of lust.

When you are in an established relationship, you shouldn't just sit back, sink into complacence, and assume he'll just love you unconditionally. This is true to an extent, but if you want to keep the flames burning, you have to work on maintaining that level of lust. One of the most common reasons for breakups is the old, "I love you, I'm just not in love with you." Usually what this means is "I no longer feel that lustful passion for you. I love you…but in the same way I love my family and close friends."

In a romantic relationship, love will give you stability, partnership, and acceptance, but lust will give you passion, fire, and sexual satisfaction.

While love is about accessibility and constant companionship, lust is a bit more forbidden; it's about wanting rather than having.

There are many ways to keep the lust alive in your relationship, you'll probably discover them all by just thinking about how things were in the beginning of your relationship, back when you were overcome by a magnetic force of physical attraction. Try to maintain some mystery when you can and get back in touch with your more sexual side. Instead of going to bed in a ratty tee shirt and shorts, invest in some sexy sleepwear. When you know he's coming home from work, change out of your sweats and wear something alluring. There are countless ways to bring the spark back into a relationship, so just play around and see what does the trick for you!

The Ugly Truth About Relationships

When you're single, it's easy to fall into the trap of thinking that everything will be perfect when you find the right guy. I'll admit that I was once guilty of this line of thinking. It can seem like a relationship is that one missing piece and once you have it, you will finally have it all. Then maybe you meet a guy, you click, you start dating, and all seems to be running smoothly until certain unpleasant realities of being in a relationship start to creep in, either slowly and by degrees or quickly and all at once.

Relationships take work; there is no way around that. You can be totally perfect for one another, you can love each other like crazy, you can be wildly attracted to one another, you can even be soul mates, and you will still have to work at it. When you're in a relationship, it isn't just about you anymore. Your choices, your actions, your behavior, your tone of voice, your mood and so forth, they all affect someone else (and vice versa). A relationship is a partnership, and having a partner is amazing in many ways, but it also means there is someone else in the picture who matters. And like you, he also comes with a fair amount of baggage, issues, unresolved pain from the past, etc.

When a relationship starts to get real, it can be confusing and overwhelming. You may wonder if you've made a mistake, if maybe this isn't the right relationship. You may feel wronged because *this isn't how it's supposed to be*. All relationships will hit points where you struggle, and actually, the struggles are a good thing. When handled right, they can make you even stronger as a couple. But when dealt with improperly, they can cause irreparable harm (to both you and the relationship).

Here are five not-so-fun facts you must face about being in a relationship:

1. Fights are Inevitable

Fighting with the person you love is profoundly painful, but it's inevitable and sometimes it's necessary. It can also be a brutal reality check. In the beginning of a relationship I think almost every woman has moments when she thinks: "Wow, this guy is amazing. He gets me and I love him so much, what could we ever fight about? Maybe other couples fight, but that will never be us." And you might really believe it; you might wonder what you could ever possibly fight about. But in time, this idealism gets shattered and you are forced to face some of the unpleasant realities of being in a relationship.

It's important to realize that even the most compatible couple will sometimes disagree, and these disagreements can escalate into arguments and full-fledged fights.

Your goal shouldn't be to never fight; it should be to fight better. Learn to fight in a way that brings about resolution rather than dissolution. A fight doesn't have to include yelling and screaming and slamming doors and hurling insults and trying to make the other person feel as bad as they made you feel. It is very difficult to come to a place of resolution when emotions are running hot, so one of the best tips to fight better is to stop discussing an issue until both of you have had the chance to reset your systems back to neutral. Whenever a conflict emerges, it is also helpful to remind yourself, and each other, that you are both on the same team and that you should try to work with each other instead of against each other.

2. The First to Say Sorry is Actually the Stronger One.

This point picks up where I left off in the first reality check. You and he are on the same team and you're fighting for the same cause, the cause being to have a healthy, happy, loving, mutually fulfilling relationship. When you make yourself the victim and him the victimizer, you aren't on the same team, you are opponents locked in a battle to prove that you're right and the other person is wrong. This puts the other person on the defensive, and he may launch a counterattack that only confirms for you that he is completely at fault, and from there it spirals into an ugly place.

Maybe you're right and maybe you do want to "win" the argument, but if you end up tearing each other down to do it, then you both lose.

Sometimes, you just need to suck it up and say, "I'm sorry we fought" or "I'm sorry you were hurt." Maybe you think he's being irrational and you don't think he's justified in feeling the way he's feeling, and maybe you're right, but it doesn't matter who's right. What should matter more is the fact that the person you love is hurt, and you can be sorry for hurting him even if you don't fully understand where he's coming from.

If he did something that hurt you, try to express that to him in a way that doesn't make him feel attacked. This is totally achievable when you're coming from a place of genuinely wanting the relationship to work and wanting to connect and share your perspective with him so the relationship will improve, and not from a place of trying to be the victor.

Sometimes he'll do something that hurts you, and you'll think he was completely in the wrong, while he'll think you're in the wrong for being upset. I'm not referring to clear-cut wrongdoing like cheating, but something along the lines of you had a bad day and wanted to spend time alone with him, but he already had plans and didn't want to cancel. You may feel he should prioritize you and cancel those plans, but he doesn't like to be the kind of person who flakes when he says he's going to do something. It doesn't matter who is right and who is wrong, and in reality, both people are usually a little of both. Trying to prove your case will get you nowhere.

3. Resentment Will Crop Up

Resentment is by far the number-one relationship killer. Resentment is what causes couples to fall out of love, to stop desiring one another, to fight constantly over everything. As a relationship progresses, the number of minor hurts will accumulate. That time he blew off date night to hang out with his friends…that time he forgot about important plans…that time he said something hurtful…that time you had a fight and he didn't say sorry…

Whether your relationship survives and blossoms or deteriorates and implodes comes down to what you do with all those hurts. In a relationship, you will get hurt sometimes, even if you're with the sweetest, most loving man in the world. He usually won't mean it; he may not even realize something he said or did was insensitive or hurtful. Maybe you say something about it, maybe you don't. Sometimes you can get over something on your own (especially if it was something innocent that you overreacted about because of your own insecurity), sometimes an apology is necessary, and sometimes a serious "relationship talk" is needed.

If you don't deal with your hurts properly, they will build up within you and morph into resentment. Once the seeds of resentment have been planted, every minor thing he does will feed them and cause them to grow, even the things that you know objectively aren't that big of a deal. The more resentment grows, the more it will poison the relationship.

You may silently punish him in retribution, which will cause him to feel resentful towards you, which will cause you to feel more resentment towards him. This is how the vicious ugly cycle begins, and things get very complicated very fast.

Sometimes you will be extremely hurt. Even if he apologized in the most sincere, loving way, you won't be able to fully forgive and definitely won't forget. You may appreciate the apology, you may accept it, but in your mind you may be thinking, "I still can't believe he would say something like that! How could he?!" So it's still there, it's still with you, and the next time an issue comes up, you'll use it as ammo against him.

When you've been hurt you are faced with a choice: hold onto it and stay hurt, or just let it go. Maybe a part of you believes he doesn't deserve your full forgiveness, maybe you don't think he deserves to get your full love and affection, maybe you're still hurt. That will happen sometimes, but you need to realize that holding onto these bad feelings doesn't help you or your relationship. They keep you stuck in a negative place instead of moving forward, and if you can't move past a conflict then you will forever be in it, and who wants that? Even if he doesn't "deserve" to be fully forgiven, make the choice to just let it go and realize that working on improving things in the future is much better that staying angry over what happened in the past.

Again, I should mention that certain things are unforgivable and I'm not talking about those things. I'm not talking about cheating or violence or something purposefully done out of malice. I'm talking about the small little hurts that rack up over time. They are the shades of grey, not the black and whites.

4. It Will Be Challenging at Times

Relationships take work, there is no way around it. A relationship is like a plant; it needs proper, consistent care or it will wither and die. And sometimes it will be really tough. There will be times when you can't seem to communicate, times when you feel disconnected and angry, times when you start to question everything. These times will become few and far between if you put in the right amount of work. This includes releasing resentments from arguments past, letting go of the need to always be right, and realizing that certain issues won't ever be resolved and you're beating a dead horse trying.

A relationship is a partnership; it's two people coming together to share a life together. However, these two people once had very separate, individual lives. They have different likes and preferences. They have different ways of dealing with things. They have different needs, different perspectives, and different values. Sometimes two people will be very compatible and will have the same views on where to live, what to spend money on, etc. For other couples, it will take a little more effort to bridge the gap.

The challenging aspects of a relationship subside when both people learn the importance of compromising and learning to see the world through their partner's eyes. You won't ever be able to inhabit his perspective, but you can try to understand it and validate it, and this is what builds a cohesive unit, when both people face challenges together instead of from opposite sides of the ring.

5. Sometimes, You're the Problem

This just might be the hardest reality check of all. Nobody wants to be the problem. It's much easier to blame someone else than admit you have issues to deal with, because dealing with issues is unpleasant and requires hard work. It's easy to blame someone for making you feel a certain way, but the reality is that oftentimes, you already felt that way. If you blame your boyfriend for "making you" feel insecure, you probably already feel insecure and because of that interpreted something innocent he said or did as critical.

We all have a certain degree of baggage, and most of our issues will rise to the surface in a relationship because love touches the deepest, most rarely accessed parts of our beings. Sometimes this can be beautiful and euphoric and other times it can be very painful because it brings up feelings and issues that we would rather not deal with. And so sometimes rather than dealing with them, we blame our guy for making us feel that way.

I'm not saying he's never at fault; sometimes he might be insensitive or hurtful (hopefully unintentionally). The point I'm making is that it's important to try to identify where the issue is really coming from. Is it him or is it you? Is he really not making you feel secure in the relationship or do you have some deep-seated intimacy issues to deal with? Does he really not make you feel loved, or do you not love yourself, and as a result are unable to let any love in from the outside?

The first step in having a healthy relationship is always to work on being your best self. This means being honest with yourself, looking at who you are and who you want to be, and dealing with anything that is getting in the way of that. Your partner can help you get there, but he can't do it for you. Only you control your emotional well-being.

Relationships can be tough at times, but when you're with the right partner, the work is so worth it. A healthy, loving relationship can enhance your life enormously and help you become your absolute best self. The path there isn't always smooth, but it is unquestionably worth it.

When Love Goes Wrong: Toxic Relationships

Something I and many other women know a lot about is toxic relationships. A toxic substance is something that causes damage to you, drains you, depletes you. A toxic relationship operates exactly like this and can irrevocably damage your sense of self.

There are toxic relationships and then there are toxic relationships, and Eric and I were in the latter.

It was only when the relationship inevitably imploded that I was able to see just how toxic the situation had been and how badly it had damaged my sense of self. Part of the reason I didn't see it sooner is that I didn't know what to look for. I let my strong feelings for him blind me to everything else. My friends tried to warn me that this was a bad situation, and so I stopped talking to them. My gut told me this was a bad situation, and so I stopped listening to it. I did what many do.

I chose not to see things as they were and instead focused on how I wanted things to be. I minimized all that was bad and clung tightly to whatever scraps of good I could find, and that was all I needed to keep going.

The pain stayed with me long after the relationship was over, and those wounds took a very long time to heal. The trouble with toxic relationships is that they aren't always so easy to identify when you're in them, and sometimes it can even feel like you're being a drama queen to call it "toxic."

Maybe you think you're experiencing the typical ups and downs that relationships bring, or maybe you blame some external source and think that as soon as it gets resolved, everything will be fine.

Being able to see a situation for what it is and accept that it isn't going to change can be empowering. It gives you the ability to look at things through an objective lens and make a decision that is in your best interest. To help you get there, I have identified the five biggest signs that you're in an emotionally toxic relationship.

1. You Never Feel Good Enough

You feel like nothing you ever do is quite right and are constantly trying to prove your worth. You become addicted to his validation. Whenever you do something and it generates any sort of approval from him, you feel relieved and it gives you just enough rope to hang onto. You try even harder to get more of that feeling, then feel like a failure when it doesn't come. No matter how hard you try, you never feel like you're enough or like you're doing things right. You live in a constant state of unease, of second-guessing yourself, of trying to be better and good enough.

2. You Can't Be Yourself

One sign that you're in a healthy, loving relationship is the feeling that you can just *be*. A big sign that you are in an unhealthy, toxic relationship is the opposite, the feeling that you can't be yourself. Instead, you have to walk on eggshells and monitor everything you say and do. You feel like you need to think twice before you speak and that certain topics are off limits, that you have to act a certain way. You are afraid to bring things up to him because you don't know how he'll react, and saying nothing is better than saying something and having him get angry. So you suffer in silence and hope that things will change, that somehow this relationship will magically transform into a healthy, happy one.

You may not even recognize the person this relationship is turning you into. You wonder why you're not the same cool, fun, confident girl anymore, and maybe your friends and family feel the same. But you love him and you've invested this much into the relationship and you reason that as soon as you get through this rough patch, you'll go back to being that girl again…

3. He Puts You Down

This is one of the biggest signs of a toxic relationship, and it seems like it would be pretty black and white, but often you don't even realize all the ways he's putting you down because it can be done in sneaky ways that aren't flat-out criticisms. And if you're in far enough, you already aren't feeling like yourself and aren't feeling good enough about yourself, so you may even agree with the negative things he says to you and about you.

Relationships are a chance for enormous personal growth. Sometimes our less-than-stellar qualities are brought to the surface and they need to be dealt with. However, there is a huge difference between a partner who can point out your flaws in a loving way, a way that encourages you to grow, and a partner who does it from a place of contempt. In a healthy relationship, he will accept you for who you are. He will love the good and accept the bad because we're all human and we're all flawed, and bad qualities just come with the territory. Anyone expecting perfection in a partner is paving the way for a lifetime of disappointment.

In a healthy relationship, you will want to improve because you genuinely want to be your best self—for your sake, for his sake, and for the sake of the relationship. You will feel loved and accepted for who you are, and both you and he will understand that change takes time, so you won't feel bad about succumbing to some of your negative qualities from time to time.

In a toxic relationship, you won't feel accepted, your partner will have little tolerance for your negative qualities, and he may shame you and belittle you for them.

I remember in an early toxic relationship with a guy, he told me that the reason he chose me was because he knew he could never "breed with" (yes, that's a direct quote) someone like me because I wasn't really wife and mother material (mind you, I was a 20-year-old college kid), so it made him feel safe knowing that this relationship wouldn't be forever. Your jaw may have dropped reading that, and maybe you're thinking "Well of course she left him after that," but I didn't! I remember feeling shame and embarrassment that I liked to go out and drink and party (again, I was 20!), and I made it my mission to prove to him what a nurturer I could be. I was always on a mission to prove something to him, I could never just be.

In a toxic relationship, put-downs run rampant. Some are overt and others are masked and both will make you feel bad, but you may not fully recognize the long-term internal damage they are causing.

4. You Fight Dirty

Couples fight, even the happiest ones, it just comes with the territory. Fights can occur over all sorts of things, both big and small. Happy couples aren't ones who never fight, they are ones who use fights and disagreements as a means to *resolve the issue.* If something can't be resolved, they learn how to communicate better and reach a place of deeper understanding.

Toxic couples usually fight to win. They use fights as an opportunity to tear the other person down, to hit below the belt, to get out all the anger and resentment they feel. Dirty fights are a sign that the resentment level in the relationship has hit its limit. These fights are full of hostility and contempt, and each person is overcome by the desire to "win" and prove their case rather than work together to lovingly resolve the issue.

5. He Won't Work on It

He doesn't take responsibility and instead blames you and makes it all your fault. (He says things like, "Well I wouldn't get so angry if you weren't always on my case!") In a toxic relationship, you feel like the problem. He doesn't value your feelings or your needs. If you're upset, it's because you're too "sensitive" or "emotional" or "irrational." He may say he's sorry, but he doesn't really own up to anything and thinks if you have a problem with the relationship then it's just that, *your* problem. He doesn't want to talk about it or work on it or try to change.

The most important quality to look for in a partner is someone who is willing to work on it. Even toxic relationships can be repaired if both people are committed to working on it. However, if he refuses to change or to try to understand your feelings and your needs, then there is nothing that can be done and your only choice is to leave.

What makes this so hard is that a guy with toxic qualities usually also has a lot of really good qualities, and we think if we try hard enough we can draw those positive qualities out even further and inspire him to change and be a better man. It rarely works that way; the only way people change is if they recognize there is a problem and they want to fix it. And no matter how many positive qualities he has, the only one that matters is a desire to make the relationship work. If he doesn't have that, then everything else is useless.

Remember This

Most of us have faulty ideas about love that originate in messages from mainstream media, our family life, or our first major relationship. (Sometimes it's a combination of all three!) True love isn't what most people think it is. It can be amazing and transformative, but only when both people are emotionally healthy and ready and willing to work on a relationship.

3

What Prevents You from Finding Love

You cannot make someone love you. You can only make yourself someone who can be loved.

– Derek Gamba

Every single girl will at some point find herself asking this question: is there just no one out there for me, or am I the problem? And girls who perpetually feel dissatisfied in their relationships might wonder if the love they want actually exists, or if they're being delusional.

The fact is, finding the right person is a matter of being the right person. And you can be just as lonely (or even lonelier) in a relationship as you are when you're single. Most women spend a significant amount of time looking not only for love, but the right kind of love. They believe they'll know it when they see it (or feel it), but don't quite know how to get it.

In this chapter, we'll look at some of the most common stumbling blocks that prevent you from getting the love you want...some are sneakier than you think. This chapter isn't just for the single and dissatisfied; even if you're married you'll gain valuable insights into how to make your relationship even better.

The Real Reasons You Can't Find Love

Being single for a certain amount of time has its benefits. I personally experienced the most growth and self-awareness during my years as a single girl, and while there were some painful and lonely moments, they all led me to a place where I could break through some of my walls and do some necessary inner work.

At the same time, most people don't make it a goal to be single forever. Most of us want love and a partner to share our lives with, but we mistakenly go about trying to attain this thing we want so much in all the wrong ways. We continue to live life in the same way and hope that it will somehow lead to different results. We know that this doesn't really make any sense, and yet we continue to operate from our ingrained default setting.

Being single isn't a curse and being in a relationship isn't a cure-all. No matter what stage of life you're in, it's important to take a personal inventory—to look at the habits and choices that are helping you and the ones that are hurting you. It's not a matter of putting yourself out there more or of signing up for every dating site and side-swiping app—finding a truly amazing, healthy relationship is much more about being ready for such a relationship. It's about identifying faulty patterns and thought processes that may be blocking you from getting what you want.

To solve a problem, you need to understand it. So let's look at some of the main reasons why you might still be single when you don't want to be, and what you might unknowingly be doing to push love away. (And before we begin, I just want to say my goal isn't to shame or blame anyone. I'm not trying to place all the blame on you; I'm just going to discuss some of the most common areas I've seen women go wrong in their quest for love.)

1. You're Too Needy

There's no faster way to repel a man than to need him. Wanting a man is not the same as *needing* one.

Neediness is a state of mind where you feel incomplete, or have an emotional void, and try to fill this empty space with a relationship or male validation. A lot of women confuse men's aversion to neediness with men's supposed aversion to commitment. But men aren't commitment phobes (at least, the majority are not). A man will happily enter into a relationship with a woman who *sees* and *appreciates* him for exactly who he is. Conversely, a man will run far away from a woman who sees him as an opportunity to feel good about herself or fill some void.

A guy wants to feel *chosen* by a woman he had to *earn*. He doesn't want to feel like he's just filling a spot that could have easily gone to any other man with a pulse.

Solution: Neediness usually stems from a lack of self-esteem or sense of worth. You feel like something is missing within yourself or in your life and erroneously believe a relationship will be the cure. If you were unhappy before the relationship, you'll be unhappy in it. Instead of feeling sorry for yourself about being single, work on your relationship with yourself. Work on feeling your best and looking your best. When you are the best you that you can be, you won't be able to keep men away!

2. You're Too Picky

Most women are usually at one extreme or the other: desperate and willing to put up with anything, or too picky and unwilling to "settle" for anything less than their dream man.

In this day and age, we're saturated with unrealistic love sagas and have developed an idea of what love *should* be and not of what love *is*, as I discussed in chapter two. We're told that love conquers all, but in truth love alone does not make for a good and healthy relationship. (I mean, just about every divorced couple loved each other at some point.) We want to be swept off our feet and taken over by this all-consuming feeling of euphoria and harmony. If we're not feeling the intensity on the first date, we'll write the guy off and say there was no "spark."

Another problem is that most women have adopted a sometimes inflexible idea that it's "better to be alone than to settle." Taken to an extreme, this mindset causes many women to close themselves off to guys with amazing traits just because of some superficial flaw that rules him out as their dream guy. The longer you're single, the worse this can get because you might start telling yourself, "Well I've waited this long to find the one, I am *not* compromising on anything and deserve to get exactly what I want!"

It's OK to have standards and to have an idea of the kind of guy you want to be with, but it's also important to be a little flexible and realize that you might not get every single thing you want, and that doesn't mean you're settling.

Maybe you don't like his job, maybe you don't like the way he dresses, maybe you think his hobbies are lame. This all might be true, but it's important to realize that these things don't tell you *who he is*, and who he is might be a really wonderful, kind, caring person.

Solution: Make a list of three non-negotiable qualities you need in a man. This does not include things like how much money he makes or how far back his hairline is. Money won't make for a happy marriage, and neither will a full head of hair, a chiseled jaw, or six-pack abs. Obviously you want to be attracted to your husband, but try not to get so caught up in the physical details. Also jot down three deal-breakers. This will help you gain clarity and perspective and take you away from relying on the long dating checklist you may have formed in your mind.

Next, when you go out with a guy and don't feel that all-consuming spark, don't write him off. Unless there was something that absolutely repulsed you about him, give him another shot. A lot of women are way too quick to dismiss a guy before really giving him a fair shot. I know more stories than I can even count of women who went on a few *meh* dates with the men they eventually married. Who knows where they would have ended up had they not given their future husbands another shot.

My husband doesn't have some of the main qualities that I used to swear up and down I couldn't live without. Through our relationship, I can now see how the type of guy I thought I wanted would have been a disaster when paired with my personality type. I, like most people, thought I knew myself way better than I actually did. Now every day I realize, with increasing awe, just how wrong I was about what I thought I needed, because I am with a person who couldn't be more suited for me.

When you open your mind just a bit, you might find yourself very pleasantly surprised!

3. You Haven't Worked on Yourself

The number one way to attract love is to make yourself into a vessel that can receive it.

A successful relationship comes down to two things: the right person at the right time. The first thing that's important to remember when it comes to relationships is that in general, like attracts like. That is, what you are or think you are is what you will attract.

If you don't value yourself, you will go for someone who doesn't treat you well, and you will be OK with it because he's just validating how you feel about yourself.

If you are emotionally unavailable, you will attract a guy who is emotionally unavailable. Now, you can want to be in a relationship and at the same time be unavailable in your own way. If you're afraid of getting hurt or feel like the guys you want always leave you, then you might subconsciously be putting up walls to protect yourself.

In order to attract a real relationship, you first need to make sure that you are in the right place emotionally. Make sure you want a relationship for the right reasons, not just to fill a void or make you feel better about yourself. You also need to develop a firm sense of who you are and learn how to be happy without a relationship.

It may seem like finding a great guy who likes you and sticks around, whereas the others couldn't or wouldn't, will take the sting out of past rejection, but it doesn't work that way. If you're still holding onto hurt from the past, then it will spill over into you relationships in the present.

Good self-esteem attracts someone capable not only of healthy interactions but of loving you for who you are. If you're not sure of yourself inside, you'll seek validation outside.

Solution: I have a friend who asks herself every day: "Would I want to date me today?" I think it's a pretty amazing exercise and will help you realize where you're falling short and what you need to work on.

If you want an emotionally healthy, confident, stable guy, then you need to make sure you mirror those qualities at the same level. I mean, why would a guy like that want to be with someone who is an insecure emotional mess? If you want that kind of guy, you need to be that kind of girl.

As soon as you're in that place where you are your best self and you mirror the qualities you want, you'll notice an instant change in your love life; you'll find that you can easily get the kind of guy and the kind of relationship you've always wanted. This path with be different for everyone, but try as best you can to discover the best path for you.

4. You Want Guys Who Don't Want You

One of the biggest obstacle standing in your way and stopping you from having the relationship you want is wanting the guys who don't want you. It's a ubiquitous phenomenon. Every day my inbox gets flooded with questions from women plotting and strategizing to capture a man who does not seem to want to be captured...at least not by her.

I am an expert on the subject because for far too many years the only guys who held any sort of intrigue for me were the ones I couldn't quite have. And the ones who were head over heels in love with me and willing to do anything for me? Blech, I didn't want them. I wanted to want them and everything they offered, but I just didn't. And the heart wants what the heart wants, right?

Before I started dating my husband, I dated a guy I'll call Kevin. Kevin was yet another classic case of the type of guy I just couldn't seem to resist. He was charming, charismatic, confident, fun, and always slightly beyond my grasp. He also had some deep-rooted emotional problems to deal with and some major commitment issues.

He was a classic "damage case," a guy who has a lot of potential hidden under a pile of issues. The "bad boy" who needs to be saved. And like many women, I wanted to be his healer, to be the woman who inspired him to break through his walls and finally commit.

Damage cases are like a pair of super sexy shoes that are brutally uncomfortable. When you look at them they're amazing—they're beautiful and sexy and you have to have them. But when you wear them you're in agony. Then you take them off and experience euphoric relief, the most incredible feeling. But this feeling doesn't come from gaining something positive, it comes from removing something negative—pain. This experience is the same as dating an unavailable guy.

He seems to be everything you want, so enticing you can't resist him. But when you have him, you just feel pain and discomfort. Your stomach is in knots as you wait for the next text, or for a sign that he truly cares. Then he gives you some sort of indication that he does, and you're ecstatic; you feel a rush of euphoria. But then he pulls back again and you're back in those unbearable shoes. Then he comes back, and relief. And on and on it goes.

When I was younger I kept chasing the high of removing those painful shoes. And I thought if only X would happen, then I would have that taking-shoes-off feeling forever. As I got older, I realized I didn't want to be on this roller coaster ride anymore. I decided that a comfortable pair of shoes that gave me the support I needed and a steady feeling of ease was much better than a sporadic shocking jolt of relief.

Kevin was the catalyst for this realization. It had been a while since I'd chased after a damage case, and I thought I'd nipped that problem in the bud until he came along and got me all twisted like a pretzel. It was devastating on many levels, especially to my ego! I mean, I was supposed to know better at that point—I was a relationship expert for crying out loud!

Solution: After a series of letdowns, of high hopes and thinking things would be different, followed by crushing disappointment and feeling like a fool for once again thinking the same story would have a different ending, I made a firm resolution to end this cycle for good. To make a lasting change that would lead me to the kind of love and relationship I really wanted. I was going to finally figure out why I kept going after the guys who didn't want me.

After being crushed by Kevin yet again, I decided to sit down and ask myself some really tough questions. What was I getting out of this relationship? Why was I so drawn to him even though I objectively knew he wouldn't be a good long-term partner? What had he even given to me? I did a lot for him, but what had he ever actually done to show me he cared? (The answer was nothing.)

I was getting nothing out of the relationship except for quick shots of temporary validation whenever he seemed to reciprocate my interest, and that is just so very sad. And then I realized that I am not the kind of woman who needs that sort of thing anymore. Maybe I did when I was younger, but I'm not that girl anymore, and I don't need to repeat history in order to subconsciously mend some old wounds.

Next I looked at why I kept going back to Kevin even though it was clear that the relationship was a dead end. I thought long and hard about what I was getting from him that kept drawing me back in, and the answer went beyond validation. I realized that with Kevin I felt less alone and maybe a little understood. Like me, he was a little lost and hurt, and that made me feel better in my own world of lost and hurt.

I also considered what I was giving to the relationship (if you could even call it that) and why. Why was I so invested in solving his issues? Why was I so wrapped up in getting inside his head? The reason, I believe, is that getting lost in his drama was an escape from dealing with my own. I had a reprieve from my own life and my own issues, one of which was why

I was so drawn to damage cases like Kevin! I felt like I had a mission and a purpose, and that felt kind of nice…at least for a little while.

Once I saw the situation for what it was, it lost all appeal for me. Instead of feeling sorry for myself because I couldn't get him to commit in the way I wanted, I felt sorry for him for having so many issues, issues that prevented him from committing to a great woman he had right in front of him.

Soon after I processed all of this and healed, my high-school sweetheart, the one I'd never quite gotten over, resurfaced. On our first date I could tell by the way he was looking at me that he was already smitten, that he had graduated from being a damage case (back when he was 17) to husband material, that he was taking me and this seriously, and that I could trust him. There was no hunt, no chase, no guessing games. I knew how he felt; I didn't even have to ask, it was just so obvious. And I knew I was cured from my damage case addiction because the fact that he wanted me didn't turn me off. Instead it made him even more appealing.

And now we're married! (And in case you're wondering, Kevin is still as single and afraid of commitment as ever…no hard feelings though, I still run into him here and there, and we're friendly. I can't help but laugh to myself when I think about all the inner turmoil he caused…although he was also the catalyst that got me emotionally ready to be in a relationship with my husband, so maybe I owe him a thank you!)

Remember, damage cases are a waste of time and energy. Wanting a guy who doesn't want you is a tragedy. Time is a precious thing to waste, so get to work and undo the faulty wiring that leads you to the guys who can't appreciate you.

More than anything else, the path that leads to lasting love involves making yourself a vessel to receive love. If you only want guys who can't want you back then you are blocked, so make the decision, right here and now, to push yourself to break free and clear away all the obstacles preventing you from getting what you truly want.

5. Faulty Filter Systems

A bad filter system sets you up for failure before your relationship has a chance to get off the ground, if you even get that far.

Everyone has a certain ingrained filter system. This system is partially due to genetic wiring, but it is largely shaped by our experiences. This filter system is often based on our interests, desires, and fears. For instance, if you are afraid of rejection, all you'll pick up on is being rejected. A hundred people can tell you how great and wonderful you are, but it won't sink in. All that will stand out to you is the one person who didn't seem to be interested in you.

If you put ten people in a room and have them listen to a class and then ask them at the end what the class was about, you'll get ten different answers. The reason is we hone in on things that appeal to us and serve our interests in some way and ignore the rest. And what is focused on and what is ignored varies from one person to the next.

So how does this affect your relationships?

Your reality is created in large part by your filter system. If you believe that the guys you want will never want you, you will find a justification for this fear even if it's far from the case. Once you come to expect the behavior, you create a self-fulfilling prophecy.

Whether consciously or not, you will start to behave in a way that turns men off (this can be very subtle and might not come across in anything you say or do), thus feeding into your original fear. If you are afraid your boyfriend will never commit in the way you want him to, you will ignore all signs of his commitment and will only focus on the signs that he doesn't want to commit. Your fear will manifest itself in behavior like clinging more tightly to the relationship or being on guard for its inevitable end, which will, in turn, cause the relationship to unravel. (I'm not talking about situations where a guy clearly won't commit, like a guy not calling you his girlfriend after an extended period of time. I'm talking about more subtle signs.)

If you believe you're unattractive, you will dismiss everyone who compliments your appearance and will write it off as them just being nice. When someone says something that implies they don't find you attractive, you'll grab hold of it and will use it as proof of your original belief.

We have an innate need to justify our thought patterns, even if these patterns don't serve us in a positive way.

Want proof? Close your eyes and pick a color. Visualize the color in your mind, picture items that are that color, see yourself dressed in that color, think about the emotions that color evokes. Spend about 30 seconds to a minute doing this and then open your eyes, what's the first thing you saw? I guarantee it will be that color unless you did this in an all white room. If we dwell on something, even for under a minute, our mind becomes programmed to pick it up.

We're all wired to look at the world in subjective ways. Reality is not objective; it is shaped by both what happens to us and how we interpret the things that happen to us.

Solution: In order to have more success in love and relationships, you need to adjust your filter system so that you see the good all around you. You need to be able to appreciate and acknowledge the goodness that is in you and in your relationship. If you let your fears run the show, you will set yourself up for sabotage.

First, you need to weed out faulty thought patterns. Anytime a negative thought pops into your mind (I'll never find a boyfriend...I'm going to end up alone...Men always leave me), pluck it out and tell yourself the opposite. This applies not only to relationships, it applies to and can be used to enhance all areas of your life. Our thoughts have a huge impact on the way we feel, and since we can control what we think our thoughts are a very powerful tool once we start using them.

I am also a big fan of keeping a gratitude journal. Every day jot down 1-2 things you're grateful for (and pick different things every day). This will re-train your brain to focus on the good. Maybe it sounds cheesy, but I've done this exercise and I recommend it to readers all the time, and the results are truly transformative.

6. The Ex Factor

Most of us are unaware of all the ways our past can bleed into our present—and even our future—if left unchecked.

I have been hurt a lot over the years, for which I am thankful. The pain has served me well in that it's given me invaluable insights into relationships (and provided me with a plethora of content to write about!) but I also came to a point where I realized the extent to which I never fully processed and let go of some of that toxic baggage.

They say time heals all wounds, but I find that is only partially true. Time makes you forget or it makes the memories more distant, but it doesn't automatically heal the wounds left behind. Healing from a devastating breakup isn't a passive process; it is something you need to actively work on.

A relationship is going to unfold in only one of two ways: it will either last forever or it will fall apart. In order to get the relationship that lasts, you have to come to terms with all the ones that didn't.

When I first started dating my husband, even though I felt very sure about his intentions I had a really tough time fully trusting him and the relationship. More importantly, I had a hard time trusting myself and my own judgment. Even though I knew my fears had absolutely nothing to do with him, I couldn't get past them.

I knew these feelings were coming from me because he did nothing to make me think he was anything other than fully committed to making the relationship work. But sometimes seemingly small, innocent things would trigger my fears and insecurities. For example, anytime he would try to reassure me by saying "I'm not going anywhere," I would feel my guard reflexively come up and I would become a bit more distant, withdrawn, and uneasy. He was understandably hurt by this and thought I didn't believe him or didn't trust him, but that wasn't it.

With a little self-reflection I was able to pinpoint exactly why it was happening. You see Eric used to say that line anytime my insecurities would flare up. And I believed him. Those words gave me an instant feeling of calm and security (it never lasted long because it wasn't the right relationship, *at all*), but it did assuage my fears temporarily. Even though the relationship was far from ideal, I believed he would never leave. I believed he couldn't live without me, just as I couldn't possibly live without him or fathom a world without him in it.

The relationship had its ups and downs ... and even though the downs were becoming more frequent and long lasting, I believed we would power through it. I believed we were in it together and would make it work. But we didn't. Instead, my greatest fear became a reality... he left me for someone else and showered her with all the love he had been incapable of giving me. Saying I was devastated doesn't do justice to the state I was in. Rather than process what had happened, I partied like there was no tomorrow. I made sure to leave no open space for the pain to slip in. I was going, going, going, no time to stop. No time to think, or worst of all, feel.

In the years that followed, I became hardened and my once open heart was now unable to feel anything for any man I dated. One by one they would fall hard for me, but I would feel nothing. There were a few guys who managed to stir something inside of me, and I would inexplicably fall hard and fast. My stomach would be in knots waiting for the next text, I would endlessly analyze everything he did to determine whether or not he liked me, I would constantly plan and plot what I would say and do to win him over. But nothing ever came from those "relationships"—save for me being left devastated—because the only guys who could get me to feel anything were the emotionally unavailable ones.

My objective mind couldn't see this, though, because my attraction to these guys was rooted in my subconscious. My last relationship had instilled a belief in me that I was unworthy of love, that I would never get the guy I wanted, that no man would love the real me ... so I sought out guys who weren't in a place to love anyone, really, and was proven right time and time again. That's the thing about the subconscious, it always seeks validation, even if it's in the form of a painful reality.

What happened to me is something that happens to many women after a toxic relationship and crushing breakup: I internalized faulty beliefs about myself and never challenged them.

Almost a decade after the relationship that broke me, I realized just how deep the scars were. I realized I had adopted a set of beliefs about myself that was sabotaging my efforts to find the love I'd always wanted. So I decided to dig deep into the darkness to purge these beliefs. I looked at that relationship through an objective lens and realized the way it had unfolded had absolutely nothing to do with who I really am.

At the time, I thought he'd left me because I wasn't good enough ... because I was unlovable ... because I was unworthy. I also stopped trusting my own judgment. I had stayed with him even though he was clearly bad for me. I had trusted him based on the few words of assurance he would provide when I was feeling insecure, and ignored all the glaring red flags. How could I trust myself not to make the same mistake again? As a result, I became a woman who believed she couldn't trust her instincts, who couldn't trust men, who couldn't open up and be vulnerable and let anyone else in.

As I've written about before, good relationships bring all your unresolved issues to the surface. Even though I had done a lot of internal work before I started dating my husband, there was a lot more that needed to be done. It started with realizing that this relationship is the complete opposite of the last one, and I am a completely different person now, so it is absurd to think I would repeat the same mistakes.

The subconscious doesn't operate from a place of reason and logic, it operates from a place of emotion. What I needed to internalize was that even though certain things felt real (like that he was going to just leave me out of the blue one day, and I needed to be on guard at all times lest I miss some warning sign), they were not reality. Feelings aren't facts, and when you look at a situation objectively, you often see just how silly and unfounded your beliefs truly are.

Once I realized what was happening, I was able to challenge some of those old faulty beliefs and replace them with newer, happier truths. I was able to finally relax and let love in. My guy noticed the change immediately, and our relationship improved drastically.

Solution: If you've been hurt in the past, try to see if you can identify any old wounds you're still carrying around with you. Think about how you interpreted the situation at the time and see if you can spot any faulty beliefs about yourself that may have developed. Then do whatever you need to in order to correct those. It isn't always easy, but is so worth it.

The Real Reasons You're Still Hung up on Your Ex

No matter how toxic (and pointless) it is to continue pining for an ex, most women have a near impossible time letting go and moving forward. It's a big problem and big topic and I want to dive in a little deeper and look at the real reasons women have such a hard time letting go.

Let's say you had a job where you felt perpetually stressed, anxious, and miserable. You put in all you could, even if it came at the expense of your ego and sometimes, your sanity. And let's say you got fired from that job. Yes, being unemployed is scary so at first you'd feel upset and worried, but you would also probably feel relieved. You'd realize it was for the best and would be thankful that you were now free to find a job better suited to you, one where you would feel valued and appreciated. You wouldn't spend sleepless nights pining for that old job, wondering what went wrong and what else you could have done. You'd realize, with perfect clarity, that it wasn't the right place for you.

Now let's say you're in a relationship where you feel perpetually stressed, anxious, worried, and miserable. You put everything you have into making it work. You give it your all, even at the expense of your dignity and emotional well-being. You put up a good fight, but it's not enough and he breaks up with you. You were miserable with him, and now you're even more miserable without him. You spend months, maybe even years, pining away.

Unfortunately, a relationship is hard to view through the same objective lens as a job. With relationships, it's not just our emotions that get involved, it's our egos, our past pain, our childhood traumas, our insecurities, our fears. Everything gets activated, and when the bomb detonates it can take months or years to clear away the wreckage.

As a result, when a relationship ends it's not just the other person that's missing; a lot of pieces of yourself also need to be retrieved. Many people make the mistake of thinking that the reason they're so sad after a breakup is because they genuinely miss their former partner. This is true to an extent, but it's far from the whole picture. The pain we feel comes from several sources, and most have nothing to do with the ex himself.

Here are the *real* reasons it's so hard to get over him:

You Think You'll Never Find Anyone as Amazing as Him

This is the biggest breakup myth of all and the reason most people find it so hard to get over their first love. They cling to the belief that since they never experienced anything like that before, they never will again.

You convince yourself that no other man on the planet has the same qualities as him and thus you have two choices: get him back or settle for someone who will never measure up. I hope you can recognize the absurdity of this! Will you meet someone else exactly like him? No, because no two people are exactly alike. But more importantly, you wouldn't want to—you and he broke up, proving that someone exactly like him is exactly what you don't need. You won't find someone with his exact qualities … you will find someone even better and more compatible with you.

You Were Infatuated

Most people confuse true love with infatuation even though these two concepts couldn't be more different. Love is about realistically seeing who the other person is, flaws and all, and appreciating the entire picture. It doesn't make demands or need things to be a certain way, it grows and flows and creates an environment where both people bring out the best in one another.

Infatuation is about creating an unrealistic image of who the other person is and turning him in your mind into a supreme, perfect being. The biggest sign you're infatuated is not being able to find a single flaw in the other person. Infatuation usually happens because you have a void in your life that he fills. You don't feel good enough about yourself and this supreme being shows interest in you, making you feel desirable and worthy, and so you cling to him for more of that feeling.

His approval makes you feel OK … it makes you feel "good enough," at least temporarily. Since he gives you something you need so desperately, you become terrified of losing him, and then the panic sets in … *what if he loses interest? How can I keep him?*

You let him get away with as much bad behavior as he wants because you're too afraid to call him out on it and risk losing him. When he retreats, you do everything in your power to reel him back in. You're in a relationship where you're not being treated the way you want, yet you can't tear yourself away. So you stay.

Eventually it ends, leaving you more fractured and empty than before. You continue to idealize him and think that the only way you'll ever feel loved is if he comes back. But love always begins with self-love, and self-love always starts from within, it can never be attained from the outside. Until you realize this, you will remain in heartbreak's unrelenting grip.

You Sold Yourself out

This ties into being infatuated. In unhealthy relationships, we will often "sell ourselves out" in an effort to make it work. Selling yourself out means accepting behavior that you would otherwise consider unacceptable, or attempting to be someone you're not. Maybe you don't speak up anymore, maybe you aren't the same bubbly, confident person you once were, or maybe you unquestioningly put him and his needs above your own.

The emotional devastation you feel after a breakup is usually proportional to the extent you sold yourself out. When these relationships end, you will often feel like a piece of you is missing, like you aren't whole. It's a miserable, almost sickening feeling. You might feel like getting him back is the only cure, but it's not. What you need to do is look at yourself and really try to determine why you accepted such poor treatment for so long, and what steps you can take to avoid getting into a situation like this again.

You Miss the Way He Made You *Feel*

Most of the time, it's not the guy you're missing ... it's the feelings you experienced when you were with him. You miss the intimacy, the closeness, the feeling of being desired and admired. You miss the way he made you feel more than who he actually is.

There is almost always a period of withdrawal after an important element of your life is gone. Whether it's your decision to cut him out of your life or not, there will suddenly be a void, and you may feel unbalanced as you try to cope without the thing that was once there to fuel you. It's like quitting coffee or cigarettes. At first you think you'll never be able to make it through the day without your "fix." It will definitely be hard at first, but when you push past the initial discomfort, you'll find you can function just as well or even better!

When you go through a breakup, you may be missing the feeling of being loved and cared for. To fill this empty space, surround yourself with people who genuinely care about you and love you for who you are. Focus on rebuilding your life in a way that makes you feel fulfilled and content with who you are. You probably relied on him to give you a feeling of worth, and now it's time to take ownership and give yourself that feeling.

You Lost Yourself

A boyfriend can often quickly go from being a part of your life to being your *entire* life. You stop seeing your friends as much, doing hobbies you enjoy, pursuing your passions. You want to spend every free moment with him and can't pry yourself away. It feels like he's your everything ... because he is! And when "everything" leaves, you're left with nothing. You feel empty, like a piece of you is missing.

The fact is, a lot of pieces of you are missing and you need to find them; he isn't the final magical puzzle piece that can complete you. The process of finding those lost pieces of your-self starts with rebuilding your life and making it full and balanced without him. When you drop other elements of your life and have your guy fill that space, you will have a huge hole once he leaves you. Realize that this hole exists not because he was the other half of your soul, but because you threw many important elements of your life overboard.

You Took It Too Personally

A lot of the time, the pain we feel after a breakup is really the throb of a severely bruised ego. Rejection hurts. Even if it's only because of incompatibility it can still sting and make you feel like you're somehow not good enough. But sometimes two people just aren't a match, it's as simple as that. Sometimes both people can see this with perfect clarity, while sometimes only one person does.

Being single can be tough and dating can be exhausting, but neither of these options is as bad as being stuck in an unhealthy relationship. Everyone has things they want to give to and get from a relationship. If what you give is what the other person can receive, and vice versa, then it's a match. If not, then it doesn't mean either of you is bad or damaged or not good enough, it just means you're not a match, and that's OK.

Try not to take it too personally and instead realize that while this might not have been the right relationship for you, the next one very well might be, so your best bet is to mentally and emotionally move past this relationship so you can open the door for someone even better to walk through.

You're Idealizing the Past

Most women seem to develop selective amnesia after a relationship ends whereby they only remember the good times and completely ignore everything that went on the rest of the time. I'm sure you shared plenty of good times and happy memories, but that's not all that went on, or the relationship wouldn't have ended.

Be real with yourself and honest about the relationship. Remind yourself of the reasons why it *didn't* work, instead of going over what you could have or should have done differently in order to *make* it work. Chances are, it would have ended no matter what you did differently.

Breakups don't happen because of small details, they occur because the two individuals in their entirety simply weren't a match. No amount of ruminating will change this so it's best to just accept it and move forward.

A breakup can feel almost like a death ... and it kind of is. It's the death of potential, the death of all the possibilities that could have been. In the beginning you were so full of hope and optimism, two of the most uplifting and exhilarating feelings there are. And now you're having a hard time parting with those feelings and everything you'd hoped for, a hard time accepting that while what you and he shared was good, it wasn't good enough. But it's OK. Not every relationship is meant to stand the test of time so don't think of it as the end of something, think of it as just the beginning of your journey towards finding the right one.

The Secret to Getting Love That Lasts

I recently attended a friend's wedding, and it was a very happy occasion not just because weddings are always happy occasions, but because this friend in particular went through a *lot* in the love department. From coming home one day and finding her live-in boyfriend of several years in bed with another woman to getting dumped out of the blue by the first guy she really saw a future with after that cheating boyfriend, to going out with one guy after the next after the next after the next and getting nowhere.

Seeing how happy she was and how amazing she and her now husband are together was really touching and inspiring. The day before the wedding, she and I got to talking and I asked her how she knew he was the one. She replied: "I knew it on our second date. I just felt like my absolute best self around him." This is one extremely important point about relationships, one that most people overlook.

Before meeting her husband, my friend had dated a string of really incredible, high-quality guys. The pattern was that they would go out on a few dates (maybe an average of 3-5) and one after the next would pull the plug and end it.

At first she was really hurt, but eventually she just got frustrated and wanted to know why this kept happening. So she decided to be bold and find out exactly why these guys dumped her.

If she had a friend in common with the guy, she would send that person to do the investigating. If not, she would call the guy up and say in a very casual and non-confrontational way: "I want to ask you something honestly … I thought we had a good thing and I'm just curious to know why you didn't want to continue dating. I've been noticing a pattern in my life of this happening and I'm starting to think maybe it's me and would really appreciate your insights."

Because she was coming from a sincere place, she got honest answers. And pretty much every guy gave her the same answer. They all felt she was a bit too muted emotionally and they couldn't really connect with her because of it.

Once she knew the problem, she went on a mission to correct it. She bought books, attended seminars, and started seeing a therapist to work through some of her issues that she thought might be causing this block. She stopped serial dating and decided to spend some time focusing exclusively on her relationship with herself.

After a few months of hard internal work, she met the man who is now her husband.

"The one thing I wish I'd realized sooner is how important it is to work on yourself," she told me. "You really should write about this and tell your readers!"

I've mentioned the importance of working on yourself already in this book, but this is probably my favorite relationship success story so I had to share it to really hammer in the point.

The part I found the most interesting about this story is how a connection was instantly formed when my friend met her husband. I wonder if this would have been the case had she not worked on herself and still been emotionally closed off.

Personal development is a lifetime commitment. We should never, ever, stop trying to be our best versions of ourselves or stop working on improving our weak points. It's not just about getting a guy, it's about living a life that is better and more fulfilling all around.

Having an amazing guy in your life is a wonderful thing that can certainly add to your happiness, but it won't ever be the sole source of happiness in your life. Happiness is an internal state that takes time and work. It isn't something that just happens; it won't just show up at your door one day.

To get the love you want, focus on building a solid foundation of self-love. Focus on working on yourself and pushing past those walls that close you off and hold you back. Feelings are scary and being vulnerable can be downright terrifying, but confronting these feelings head on is better than living your life behind Plexiglas. What's that like? It's like sitting inside a coffee shop looking out the window at the New York City streets. You feel like you get a sense of what's going on out there, but you aren't feeling the wind in your face, you're not smelling the street meat, you aren't immersed in the hustle and bustle, you aren't filled with that pulsing energy. You are a spectator, not a participant. You're close, but not close enough to be in it. That's what happens when you hold yourself back, when you put up a plastic wall, when you live with the fears from your past, and when you take solace in the wall rather than actively working on ripping it down.

Instead of living behind it, say thank you to the wall. It served its purpose but you don't need it anymore. You are free to let yourself feel and be present and be open, and you are free to remove any obstacles holding you back.

Remember This

Being single has its benefits, but if you want to settle down you need to take a good hard look at what might be holding you back … and make a concerted effort to deal with it!

4

The Dead-End Relationship

A dead end can never be a one-way street; you can always turn around and take another road.

– Bo Bennett

Settling for what you don't want is the surest way to not get what you do want. The dead-end relationship is probably the most ubiquitous type of relationship in this day and age. Since this book is all about finding lasting love and being in a great relationship, I would be remiss if I didn't at least briefly review some of the most common complicated relationships scenarios and how to deal with them.

Dead-end relationships are largely a phenomenon that affects women. You don't often hear men lamenting over the status of their relationships, wondering where things are heading and whether or not there's a future. Yes, guys can get frustrated when they don't know if a girl is into them, but it's not the same thing. Men are really the gatekeepers of commitment, and much of the time women put themselves in a position of being along for the ride, letting men call all the shots.

A lot of women end up shackled to dead-end relationships for months…years…decades! They stay and cling to the hope that someday he'll come around and will commit. It's a huge waste of time and energy, and it really does a number on your sense of self.

Signs He'll Never Commit

Women of all ages and across all cultures are united in their quest to determine the following: Does he like me? Is he serious about me? Will he ever commit to me? Trust me, I get it. I've experienced those gut-twisting feelings, the ones that leave you with a constant sense of impending doom in the pit of your stomach causing you to question everything, including yourself.

It's understandable. I mean, there is a lot at stake when you put your heart on the line and you can end up wasting months, or years, of your life on a man who never intended to keep you around for the long haul. And the aftermath of these situations is never pretty.

So what can we do to spare ourselves the time, energy, and heartbreak that goes into determining how a man feels?

After giving this topic a lot of thought and interviewing numerous guys, I've uncovered five telltale signs that he isn't going to commit to you now or ever.

1. You Don't Know Anything Real about Him

You can talk to someone for hours and hours every day and

not know anything real about him. You might know details about his life, but you don't know who he really is, his real and true self that exists beneath all the superficial fluff.

I'll use myself as an example.

So if I was out with a guy and he asked me what I did for a living. My basic answer would be that I write about relationships. That's something that I tell anyone I meet who asks me what I do.

Now if they ask why I chose this as a profession, I'd say that I like it, it's fun, and I think (or at least I hope) I'm good at it.

Now let's go a layer deeper. Why do I write about relationships? Well, I studied psychology in college and I've always been interested in human behavior and fascinated by the dynamics of relationships.

And now a level deeper...

I write about relationships because I want to help people, and I have a vested interest in helping girls heal from heartbreak.

And now a level deeper...

I've been hurt by men in my life—I've really had my heart annihilated—and writing about relationships is cathartic. It has helped me heal from my own pain, and I've been able to help a lot of other women in the process.

Anyone can know I write about relationships, but when talking about why I do that there are many levels that go far beyond the first superficial answer.

I used this example to illustrate a larger point: there is knowing someone, and there is knowing someone.

When a guy opens up to you, when he shares his dreams, his fears, his hopes, his wishes, his motivations, etc., he is investing in you. By investing in you, he is committing himself to you. Maybe you're not official, maybe you haven't said *I Love You*, maybe he isn't proposing, but he's still committed.

We don't share ourselves with just anyone. Most of us have been burned badly enough in our lives to learn to be selective about the people we open up to.

Opening ourselves up comes with big risks. We become vulnerable and we also feel closer and more connected to the person we've revealed ourselves to.

If a guy doesn't share his true self with you, if he won't let you see who he is at his core, the chances are high that he's not in it for the long haul and doesn't see a future with you. If you're really unsure about whether or not a guy is serious about you, take a look at the things you know about him and ask yourself if you *really* know who he is. Don't panic if you don't know the real stuff yet—we'll talk about how to create a deep emotional connection a little later!

2. He Disappears for Days or Weeks at a Time, Then Acts Like It Was No Big Deal

If a guy truly cares about you, he will want to make room for you in his life. Even if he has a lot going on and won't be available for a few days, he'll send a text or message to let you know he's thinking about you.

If he takes vacations from the relationship with no warning it means he isn't worried about losing you, and this is never a good sign. If a guy knows for certain that you'll always be there waiting in the wings, no matter how badly he behaves, he won't respect you and he definitely won't want to commit to you—why should he when he knows he doesn't have to? There would be absolutely no benefit for him.

His disappearing acts serve more as a way to let you know this relationship isn't serious and he is still free to do what he wants. It's his way of letting you know that you aren't a deciding factor in where he goes and what he does.

3. He Tells You He Doesn't Want a Relationship

This seems like an obvious one, but unfortunately, it's not! In fact, I think the most common relationship in this day and age is the *non-relationship,* that is, when you're dating a guy and you're basically boyfriend/girlfriend aside from the fact that you're not.

The simple truth is this: when a guy says he doesn't want a relationship, what he's really saying is he doesn't want a relationship with *you.*

I know you think you're the exception and your situation is different. I've been there and I'm telling you, you're not and it isn't. You're like every other girl in a non-relationship. You're a great girl who maybe sold herself a little short and is in a situation where the guy calls all the shots and is just taking you along for the ride as you sit patiently in the back seat, waiting for him to decide if you're "good enough."

If he tells you he doesn't want to be in a relationship, or he has "commitment issues," or hates labels, just take it at face value, do yourself a favor, and move on.

4. He Doesn't Take You on Real Dates

If your dates consist of you going over to his place and watching a movie or you cooking for him, then he isn't taking you or the relationship very seriously.

When a guy is invested in you and cares about you, he wants to go out of his way to impress you and show you he cares. I know most women don't feel this way but trust me, when a guy likes you, it's *obvious*.

If he puts in the bare minimum when it comes to dates it means he doesn't feel like you're worth the effort. Are there exceptions? Sometimes. But even if a guy is jobless and broke and doesn't have the money to take you out, he'll find some sort of cheap and creative way to show you he cares.

When a guy cares about a girl and sees a future with her, he wants to bring her into his world as much as possible. He wants to introduce her to the things he likes: movies, music, books, hobbies. These aren't things that require much of a financial investment but they speak volumes about his level of *emotional investment*.

If you're the only one making the effort to keep the spark alive and do special things, it's a sign that he isn't very invested in you.

5. He Won't Introduce You to His Family

A lot of women make the mistake of thinking that meeting a guy's friends is a big deal. Maybe some guys view this as a big deal, but most don't. Maybe he just wants to show you off because you're hot, or maybe he just doesn't think much of introducing girls to his friends. I have plenty of friends who looked at meeting his friends as the Holy Grail...the telltale sign that he's all in, he's committed. It's not. Meeting his family is where it's at. (Side note: while meeting his friends isn't the biggest deal, if he won't introduce you to them it's a definite red flag.)

When you're in a relationship, talk of meeting the family should come up. Maybe you don't meet them right away, but he should give you some sort of indication that it's on the horizon. At the very least, he should let you know that his family is aware of your existence.

If he doesn't talk about his family, or changes the subject anytime you bring them up, it's a sign that he has no intention of making the introduction.

As I mentioned earlier, when a man is serious about a woman, he brings her into his world. By keeping you away from his family, he's essentially saying he doesn't see you being in his world for the long run.

I should point out that there are guys who introduce almost every girl they date to their families and don't really see it as a big deal...and maybe their families are used to this revolving door of girlfriends. However, if he's serious about you, he will take this meeting a little more seriously than he has in the past. He'll be excited, and maybe a little nervous about you meeting them because he really wants them to like you, and for you to like them. If he doesn't really seem to care, then even if he does introduce you to them it's a sign he isn't fully invested in having a future with you.

The Pseudo-Relationship

A pseudo-relationship can take on many forms, but in essence it's a relationship with some mutual interest and attraction but no real commitment. The lack of commitment is usually because one person is a little less interested and invested than the other. I can't even count how many of these types of relationships I've been in. If the definition of insanity really is doing the same thing over and over but expecting different results then I should have been locked away in a padded room many times over! I kept winding up in situations where I was kind of in a relationship but not really, always hoping it would turn into one, but it never did. It rarely does.

Meantime Relationships

A few years ago I met a really wonderful guy. He was my type to a T, both physically and intellectually. From the moment we met sparks started flying, conversation flowed effortlessly, and we just seemed to click.

The catch? He was way too young, like way younger than I'd ever even consider.

It wasn't even so much about the number of years between us; the issue was more rooted in the fact that we were in completely different places in our lives.

He was barely out of his teens, still in school and had yet to learn about the stresses and struggles that come with adulthood.

For me, college felt like eons ago and things like where to

EVERYTHING YOU NEED TO KNOW IF YOU WANT LOVE THAT LASTS

intern over the summer and which frat party to go to weren't on my list of priorities.

I was straightforward about the fact that a relationship between us wasn't in the cards, but he wasn't deterred.

Instead, he went on and on about how age is just a number, how he was mature beyond his years, how the gap between us wouldn't feel so large in a few years time.

And he actually made sense. So much so that I soon found myself seriously considering giving it a shot. I mean, I wasn't dating anyone else, what would be the harm? This wouldn't be a *real* relationship, it would just be for the meantime. And that my friends, is the problem.

Fortunately, I was able to snap myself back into reality fairly quickly and I put a swift kibosh on the entire situation, knowing that it would only be a matter of time before the infatuation really took hold and blocked me from accessing my objective reasoning skills.

I'm not saying the youngin' and I could never have worked. If we'd met when we were both older things might have stood a chance. But at that time, it was a no-go. (In addition to the age thing he lived in a different state…double whammy!)

In order for the relationship to really work, I would have had to wait about a year or two for him to get his life in order, and that just wasn't something I was willing to do.

So why am I telling you this?

Because this story brings up the very important concept known as "meantime" relationships. They may appear innocent, but they can cause significant problems.

This situation got me thinking about my past relationships and I was pretty struck by how many of them started as "meantimes." There were so many times when I compromised what I wanted and dated a guy even though I knew it wouldn't work because...well why not?

Many moons ago I started seeing this guy who flat out told me he didn't want to be in a relationship and that he had feelings for someone else. I was a little hurt, but not super bothered because I knew things would never work out in the long term anyway due to other factors.

Despite all this, we started casually dating. I didn't see the harm; it was just for the meantime. When someone better suited for me came along, I would just cut things off. That's easy enough, right?

Wrong! I ended up developing feelings for him during the course of our casual non-relationship, and knowing that he didn't want me in the same way only made me want him more. By that point I was in too deep so the fact that a relationship with him could never work was no longer even a blip on my radar.

Infatuation is a sneaky little bugger and once it takes hold, all rhyme and reason go out the window. The problem with "meantime" relationships is they provide the perfect environment for infatuation to bloom, then before you know it you've been left devastated by some guy you never really wanted in the first place.

Another issue with "meantime" relationships is that they usually come from an unhealthy place in you: maybe you're afraid to be alone and believe that nothing better will come along.

These deeply rooted feelings and beliefs are powerful and can cause you to abandon your better judgment. Then when things come to an end it won't matter that you weren't all that invested to begin with. The hurt and rejection will hit you just as hard if not harder because they will confirm your deeply held fears and beliefs.

Every decision we make and action we take has an impact. The people we let into our lives invariably leave an impression on our hearts, and sometimes this can be for the good while other times it can be for the not so good. (This refers to both relationships and casual hookups.)

Whether you're aware of it or not, you will also carry those impressions into your next relationships and into your interactions with men in general. Given that, it's essential to be selective about the people you choose to let in.

If you know things would never work out with a particular guy, why bother starting anything?

Life is too short to waste your time on limited-time relationships, the kind that are doomed from the start. Before you get in too deep, try to keep a clear head and an objective perspective. If you have certain deal-breakers, don't compromise on them because you're afraid of never finding what you want, because this can lead to a far worse fate.

Why is this so hard? Because dating smart isn't really a thing in this day and age (even though it should be!) Instead, we're encouraged to date around, play the field, get "experience." But this is opening ourselves up to the possibility of being heartbroken, having our trust violated, being hurt, and taking all of that into your next relationship, which could potentially ruin it.

My suggestion is to break free of the pack and date smart.

Use your objective lens that I talked about earlier. Identify your deal-breakers and stick to them!

The Placeholder Relationship

It's time to get blunt and bring on a dose of honest truth. A placeholder relationship usually occurs when a guy isn't into a girl enough to commit…but is into her enough to keep her around for companionship, emotional support, and sex.

When it comes to all things sex and companionship, a guy will say, "Sure, if you're offering…"

The problem is that this relationship isn't based purely on sex. It's not your typical "booty call" or friends with benefits arrangement. It is a step beyond that, but still isn't an official relationship.

There usually are real feelings involved in these sorts of situations and that's why girls have such a hard time letting go. They cling to the potential of what could be and can't accept things as they are. Guys are typically pretty bad at knowing whether or not they'll develop feelings for a girl they're casually involved with. And most guys won't develop real feelings for the girl as long as they never look to her for emotional support. Once a guy starts leaning on a girl emotionally, he starts becoming attached to her. Now the girl he only intended to keep around as a casual hookup, someone to help ease some of his loneliness in the "meantime," becomes this pseudo-girlfriend.

On the one hand, he cares for her and wants her around. After all, he feels better when she's there than when she's not. On the other hand, he just can't fully commit. Maybe he thinks he can do better, maybe she has some qualities that are deal-breakers to him, maybe it just doesn't feel right. He may not even be aware of the reason, there is just something holding him back. But not so far back that he leaves. So he keeps her around. He figures it's working right now, and once he gets himself together (that is, he starts actually *doing* the things in his life that he intends to do and living his life purposefully) he'll make a clean break from the non-girlfriend.

The only problem is…many men go their whole lives intending to do what they've always wanted to do but never getting around to it. When this happens to a man, he falls deep into this non-relationship.

The girl supports him emotionally so that he can find the strength to become the man he's always wanted to be. She aims to bring him comfort and relief from his inner pain and strife. But instead of being empowered, he actually becomes dependent on her and uses her as an emotional crutch. Instead of getting stronger, he gets weaker and more attached to this girl.

Months or years go by and the girl continues to hold onto the idea that if she just loves him enough, he'll be strong enough to love her back. At this point, she is also in deep. She has invested so much time and energy into him and the idea that someday things will all work out that she really needs it all to mean something.

Now we're at this point: Girl has poured months or years of love and obsession into this guy, hoping he'll one day come around. Guy has become emotionally dependent on the girl for her love and support, but he knows in his heart that the situation isn't what he actually wants and she isn't the girl for him.

How does it all end?

Typically…in heartbreak. What usually happens is that the "better thing" the guy was waiting for appears, and the moment it does he disappears.

The guy is able to get out of this situation with minimal damage. He got to enjoy a cozy, comfortable pseudo-relationship while he was sorting himself out, and now he gets to move on unscathed to something even better. He may feel a little guilty, but he can always rationalize the guilt away by saying: "Well, we were never in an official relationship. What did she think was going to happen?"

This may sound impossibly cruel, callous, and unfair, but before you throw your hands up and declare all men selfish jerks, consider this: your time is *your* responsibility. No one can make you do anything unless they're holding a gun to your head. You stayed because you were getting something out of the situation, too. The worst thing you can do to yourself is hold onto bitterness and rage. You may be justified in these feelings, but they won't serve any positive function; they will just make you hardened, angry, and jaded, and all of this will block you from meeting someone who can actually give you the relationship you want.

If you've been seeing a guy for a few weeks and everything is up in the air, just relax and let things run their course without being worried. But if you've spent the majority of your free time with a guy for the last couple of months—you eat together, sleep together, and support each other emotionally—and he's making no effort to lock you down…then you're in a placeholder relationship. What you do about it is your decision to make, but just realize that if you do nothing, nothing will change.

When a Guy Likes You...but Not Enough

One of the biggest problems in the world of dating and relationships is when a guy likes you, but not enough.

I have said over and over again that when a guy likes you, it's obvious (I even devoted an entire chapter to this statement in my last book). As in, clear as day, no room for error, no signs to interpret or messages to uncover. So then why is the most asked question: Does he like me?

I have asked this question many times myself, and it's a miserable feeling to invest your time and emotions into someone when you're not sure where he stands. Through time, experience, and research, I've learned that when you have to question how he feels...you already have your answer. He likes you, just not enough.

The problem is that so many of us get caught in a trap of trying to figure out why. We can't understand how he can say so many sweet things, how he can be so open and present when he's with us, how everything can feel so right when we're with him...yet he can't give us what we really want, which is usually a committed relationship.

Maybe he has valid reasons. Maybe he *is* under a lot of pressure at work, maybe his parents' divorce when he was a kid really *did* make him stop believing in monogamy, maybe the ex-girlfriend who cheated on him really *did* destroy his ability to trust, maybe he *is* terrified of commitment...the reasons don't matter, the facts do. And if a guy says he doesn't want to be in a relationship with you, he means it.

He probably does care about you, he does enjoy spending time with you, he does like you...he just doesn't like you enough. Maybe it's because he's incapable of liking someone past a certain point (a point that would lead to a relationship), or maybe he just doesn't see himself with someone like you for reasons beyond your control. It doesn't matter.

If he likes spending time with you and hanging out, but doesn't want to be official...he likes you, he just doesn't like you enough.

If you run into each other here and there and talk for hours and maybe even hook up, but you don't hear from him after...he likes you, he just doesn't like you enough.

If you've been seeing each other for a while and he refuses to be exclusive, or doesn't want to put a label on it...he likes you, he just doesn't like you enough.

If he isn't giving you the commitment you want...he likes you, he just doesn't like you enough.

Sadly, most women believe a man not liking them enough is a reflection on them, and they make it their problem. They think if only they did more for him, if only they were prettier, if only they could help him learn to trust again, if only they hadn't said this and instead had said that...everything would be different. It wouldn't. If this is how he feels, nothing you say or do will change that. His issues are his issues. You pave the way for a lot of unnecessary hurt when you make them yours.

When a guy shows a genuine interest in who you are and what you like, he is invested. And when he takes the information gathered about what you like and goes out of his way to give it to you, he is in love.

So stop torturing yourself with guessing games that will give you as much information as plucking petals off a rose. And stop waiting to hear the words.

Instead, look at the *actions*. Look at what he does, how he treats you, how he tries to make you happy. He may not always get it right, but that's not what matters. What matters is the intention.

When it comes to love, the rule to live by is never allow yourself to care for someone who hasn't shown he cares about making you happy. This is why it's best to keep relationships slow and steady in the beginning, it'll give you a better sense of the man you're dealing with.

The Friend Who Seems Like Something More

I get a lot of questions about the "friend zone," usually from women who are trying to break out of it and into the relationship zone.

Of all the relationship issues out there, I think this is the easiest one to address.

First, I will say I relate to the confusion. A few years ago I met a guy I thought would be perfect for me, and I was crushed when I found out he had told a friend of mine (who had suggested he ask me out) that he didn't want to date me because he was good friends with some of my good friends and didn't want things to get "weird."

I naively took his excuse as fact and was determined to show him that I was a cool girl and if he dated me, there would be zero weirdness. I made a point of letting him know that I run a website with my ex-boyfriend (talk about overcoming a weird situation!) and have stayed friends with a lot of guys I've dated in the past. I took every opportunity that presented itself to let him know that dating me carries zero weirdness. I also went on a pathetic quest to prove to him how great we would be together and to highlight how much we had in common. (I shudder thinking back on this now!)

The point is, I made a mistake that a lot of women make when a guy uses the old "I don't want to ruin the friendship" excuse. We take that as fact and believe if it weren't for that he would ask us out and we'd live happily ever after.

I'm not saying you can't ever get out of the friend zone with a guy, because it is possible in some cases, but I am saying it's a waste of time to put all your energy into trying. It's a waste of time to tally up the "signs" to try to figure out if he likes you as more than a friend because…no guy is ever genuinely concerned with ruining the friendship! If a guy really likes a girl, the last thought that will cross his mind is fear of ruining the friendship. I have posed this question to countless men and the answer is always the same: no man is ever worried about ruining the friendship with a girl he likes.

If he tells you this is his reason for not wanting to date you, he's probably just trying to spare your feelings; the real reasons is most likely that while he enjoys hanging out with you, he doesn't feel enough of a romantic attraction to want to take things further. This doesn't change even if you and he have hooked up. A hook-up (or multiple hook-ups) just means he is somewhat attracted to you, but again, not enough to want to date you. Because if he wanted to, he would.

It all goes back to one of the most essential concepts of all when it comes to dating: when a guy likes you, it's obvious.

Now there is maybe only one other reason why a guy you're friends with might like you but not ask you out, and that's if he's afraid of being rejected.

Most men are terrified of rejection and will do anything to avoid it. Getting around this one is easy enough, though—just indicate that you're interested in him. You don't need to be obvious about it, just give him something to go on, anything that lets him know he won't be rejected if he asks you out. If he knows you're interested and won't reject him and he has feelings for you, he will pursue you. There won't be any talk of ruining the friendship. It goes against a man's nature to see an opportunity to get something he wants and not take it.

What if you show him you're interested and he reciprocates, but then tells you he can't be in a relationship right now? Well then, forget it. If what you want is a relationship, don't spend time on someone who can't or won't give you that. In these cases nothing you do will talk him out of it so it's best to just stay friends and continue exploring your options.

OK, now let's review:

- No man is ever afraid of ruining the friendship.

- Plotting ways to get out of the friend zone is a waste of time and will leave you with nothing but shameful memories.

- The primary reason a guy might like you and not ask you out is that he's afraid of being rejected. All you need to do is demonstrate a small amount of interest so he knows he won't be rejected and humiliated if he asks you out.

Why We Stay in Bad Relationships

I know all too well how hard it is to extricate yourself from a bad relationship. You've invested so much time and energy into the situation and refuse to accept things as they really are.

You pay attention to the things you want to hear and disregard all the red flags because you want this relationship to mean something, and you just can't accept that he doesn't reciprocate your feelings. You cling to the belief that things would be different if only XYZ were no longer an issue.

When things are good, they are so good. When they're bad, you cling to the good memories, rationalizing reasons to stay. And you do. You stay until he goes and you're left crushed, and then the pain comes flooding in.

You may think the reason it hurts so much is because he was the perfect guy for you and you let him get away. But that's not it. I think the reasons it hurts so much when these situations end is because you're left trying to understand how it is that a smart, intuitive woman such as yourself could ignore so many blatant red flags and stay with a guy who didn't treat her right. You feel like you've sold yourself short, like you've compromised your values and gone against what you know to be true, and it's a miserable feeling.

You feel like he took something from you and now there's a void you need to fill. And he did, and you do.

He took advantage of you, he allowed you to keep investing

even though he was never on the same page. He made it seem safe for you to be vulnerable with him, and you felt understood and connected. Vulnerability is a gift, and when someone exploits that gift, it can be unbearable.

Imagine you're in the middle of Times Square and a weird, crazy-looking guy comes up to you and asks for directions. You're a nice person so you oblige, but then later notice that your wallet is missing. You are not surprised in the least—you kind of knew that would happen. Oh well, time to cancel the credit cards and order a new driver's license.

Now let's say a handsome, charming, British man approaches you in Times Square asking for directions. You're taken by his sexy accent and dreamy eyes. You chat for a while and give him the 411 on NYC and all the places to visit. He leaves and you reach for your wallet...and it's gone. You're floored. Your thought process will probably be something like this: How could I have been so stupid? I can't believe I fell for that! There must be something wrong with me...am I really that naive? I thought he was interested in me, what I fool I am! Or maybe he was just hitting on me. Maybe I dropped my wallet...

I don't think I need to spell out the difference between these two scenarios; it's pretty clear.

When we feel like we've compromised our values and better judgment, it hurts. We don't want to believe we could have been so foolish, so we try to find another reason, another explanation, one that makes us less culpable.

So why do we do it? Why do we stay in relationships when we aren't being respected, when our emotional needs get dismissed, when we feel bad about ourselves, when we're insulted, when we're essentially treated like crap? We would never tolerate such things from a job or a friendship...we would leave. But in romantic relationships we stay.

Here are some of the core reasons:

1. You Don't Want to Believe You Could Stay with Someone Who Treats You Badly

So you convince yourself that's not what's happening. I remember when I was in my really bad relationship a friend approached me and expressed her concerns. She said she didn't think he was treating me right and I should get out of the relationship. This was still early on and had I listened, I would have saved myself a significant amount of pain.

But I didn't listen. Instead I got extremely defensive and told her, and this is a direct quote, "You don't know what you're talking about—he treats me like gold!" And I really believed it. I had convinced myself that the kind things he did amounted to gold...and everything else he did could just be ignored because gold shines brighter than that stuff, anyway!

I really cared about him and didn't want to believe that someone I cared about could treat me badly, so I created a different story. In my story nothing was that bad; I was probably just exaggerating his bad behavior. He probably didn't mean those nasty things he said. He was stressed out and sad and couldn't always control his temper so none of that bad stuff counted, what counted was the good stuff!

The human mind has an extraordinary ability to write its own version of reality, and that's what mine did. It just seemed easier than accepting that maybe, possibly, I was in bad relationship.

2. You Don't Believe You Deserve Better

You may not actively believe you don't deserve better, but somewhere deep down that's how you feel. Don't dismiss the power of the subconscious mind; it is the puppet master behind almost everything we do. If you've developed a belief at some point that you are unworthy of love, then you won't attract healthy, happy love. You'll stay in bad relationships because that's what you think you deserve and what you believe to be normal. And if all you've had are bad relationships, you won't really have a basis for comparison. Since all you know is being treated like crap, then crap is what you'll come to expect.

Eventually you might figure it's better to stay in this type of relationship than have no relationship at all. You might start having a fatalistic belief that this is the kind of relationship that was just designated for you.

Obviously this is a very dangerous belief that can lead to a lot of unhealthy choices. While it would be nice to just flip a mental switch and instantly wire yourself to believe that you're worthy of love, changing deeply held beliefs about yourself takes a bit more work. But it is possible! Some can do it on their own, but working with a great therapist can really expedite the process.

3. You Have Excessive Compassion Disorder (ECD)

It might not be in the DSM, but ECD is a very real problem. Excessive Compassion Disorder is a diagnosis I came up with to explain the mostly female propensity to make excuses for a guy based on his potential rather than his current behavior. A woman's ECD kicks into gear when she sees a guy acting badly, but also thinks she sees the good guy he could be if only he got over his issues.

You make excuses for him: he had a rough childhood, he went through a bad breakup, he's depressed, he hates his job, he's in debt…whatever it is, you see that thing as the cause of his bad behavior and believe because of that it's not his fault. You figure that as soon as he overcomes that one thing, everything will be different.

Now I'm not saying you shouldn't ever give anyone the benefit of the doubt, but you need to hold people accountable for their bad behavior, even while being compassionate about the root cause for it. You also need to realize that you can't change another person, you can't get over his issues for him, you can't solve his problems, and you can't fix his life. You can inspire change and you can be there for support, but you can't do it for him. A person can only help himself. When you become his fixer, then you risk forming an unhealthy, codependent relationship.

If he isn't actively working on himself and trying to be a better man, then there is nothing you can do. Compassion is a wonderful virtue, but it needs limits, otherwise you run a real risk of having your heart broken.

If you're in a relationship where you feel bad about yourself, where you aren't being treated with respect, where you find yourself constantly making excuses for him, where other people in your life are expressing concern, where you don't even feel like yourself anymore, then it's time to take some space and do some real thinking about whether this relationship is something you need in your life.

If you have dated guys who treat you like crap in the past, or if you are currently involved with a guy you know doesn't treat you the way you deserve, ask yourself the following questions:

- What thoughts/behaviors/beliefs led you into this relationship?

- What did you bring to the relationship that was good and that you would want to use in your next relationship?

- What did you do in this relationship that you never want to do again?

- Why did you stay in this relationship even though it didn't feel good? What were you getting out of it?

- What need did he fulfill for you?

I'll get into this concept more when I talk about what ruins relationships, so keep reading!

Remember This

Men aren't that complicated. If a guy says he doesn't want to be in a relationship, he means it. If he isn't taking steps to be with you, it's because he doesn't want to. If you can't tell how he feels, then you actually already know how he feels. See? Not complicated.

5

What Ruins Relationships

To acquire love (...) fill yourself up with it until
you become a magnet.

– Charles F. Haanel

I've been writing about relationships for years and can't
help but notice patterns in where women go wrong. It's not
anyone's fault. No one sets out with bad intentions, trying to
sabotage her relationship. Usually, all a girl wants is to keep
her relationship strong and happy. She wants it to last, but
oftentimes she still ends up doing things that can push a guy
away and ruin a relationship.

One area where women go wrong is in not working on
themselves and letting less than ideal character traits go
unchecked. I think that on the one hand we'd like to believe
that this is the way we are and the person we're with should
just take it or leave it, on the other hand we realize that isn't
really the healthiest attitude, especially when it comes to negative tendencies like being jealous, perhaps the biggest
relationship-ruiner of all.

A lot of women just don't fully understand how men operate, or how a woman's behavior impacts the relationship

dynamic overall. There is a lot of misinformation out there, so many women don't know what it truly takes to have an amazing, happy, long-lasting relationship. Read on to learn what not to do.

Common Relationship Mistakes Most Women Make

Before I talk about all the things you might be doing wrong, I want to preface it by saying I don't think the woman is unilaterally responsible for the relationship and fully to blame if things don't work out. But this book is aimed at women so I'm going to address the most common relationship sins women commit. Some are sneaky and subtle, others glaringly obvious.

Being Too Me-Centered

Relationships typically fall apart when your focus stops being on the person you're with and starts shifting to you. When you focus on your own wants, your own worries, your own fears, your own needs, and pay no attention to how your guy feels and experiences things, you essentially turn him into an object and a means to an end.

When we objectify people, we only see them in terms of how they can serve us for a specific purpose. Maybe you want him to act a certain way so you will feel valuable, desirable, worthy of love. And you may feel resentment when this guy doesn't give you these things. Or you feel like you're giving everything to the relationship and getting nothing back. In that case you can't appreciate him for what he does because it's never enough—all you see is what he isn't doing.

The me-centered mindset can cause problems no matter what stage of a relationship you're in, casually dating or committed. A lot of women feel baffled when a guy suddenly seems to lose interest. This typically happens because she is coming from a me-centered place. She gets so fixated on achieving some sort of relationship goal, like being official, and on figuring out how he feels, that everything becomes about her and what she wants and needs. It seems innocent, but suddenly his interest begins to wane. When you focus on getting what you want out of the relationship, rather than on enjoying yourself and connecting with the other person, you are using the guy as a means to feel good about yourself and worthy of love, and that is not the pathway towards a meaningful connection.

Being Jealous

I get it. Maybe you've had your heart broken in the past and maybe you're trying to prevent it from being broken in the future. But panicking every time he glances in another girl's direction, going through his phone and e-mail, and interrogating him after any amount of time spent out of your vicinity is not the way to stop your heart from being broken! In fact, it is one of the fastest ways to ruin your relationship and have your man think you're completely insane.

Being paranoid that he's going to cheat will not make him less likely to cheat, but it will make you afraid and insecure, and these feelings will seep into your relationship and poison it. Oftentimes, jealousy is the result of your own insecurities. If this is the case, you must make an effort to figure out the underlying cause and get a handle on it. Other times, your guy just isn't trustworthy. Maybe he flirts with other women, maybe he has cheated in the past. If this is the case, it might be time to assess why you're with someone you can't trust.

Not Respecting His Personal Space

If he's in a bad mood or doesn't feel like talking, leave him alone and let it be. Most guys don't like to talk about their issues the way women do. Instead, they prefer to pull back and work things out internally in the proverbial "man cave." Women go about things differently. When a woman is upset, she seeks out those closest to her and wants to share with them. Don't take it personally when he doesn't want to come and cry on your shoulder. And don't take it personally when he just needs some space. It doesn't mean he doesn't like you anymore or thinks you're a nuisance, but if you badger him about taking space, then that may end up being the case.

Expecting Him to Make You Happy (and Blaming Him When He Doesn't)

No relationship will ever *make* you whole, happy, or fulfilled. That's the little-known fact about relationships that no one likes to talk about because it's not as romantic as the idea of someone else coming into the picture and filling your life with sunshine and rainbows.

The truth is that you need to come into a relationship

already happy, fulfilled, and whole, and then allow that to spill into the relationship. Happiness is something you put into your relationship, not something you get out of it. A relationship can certainly add to your overall happiness, but it can't be the sole source of it.

Being Passive-Aggressive

Men are much more straightforward than women. If you're not straightforward and tell him nothing's wrong and then pout and mope around waiting for him to press you further, you'll just cause anger and resentment to build. Be honest and straightforward with him if you have an issue. When you drop hints and expect him to pick up on nuances, you're setting him up to fail and setting yourself up to get even more upset and angry. Most men just don't pick up on subtleties like women do. Maybe you take it to mean he doesn't care or doesn't pay attention, but that's just the way he's wired.

Nagging

No guy is perfect and no man is capable of giving you every single thing you need. There will be times when you're not happy with something he's doing. If this happens, *do not* nag him over it. The best strategy is to tell him what you want (I love it when you do X) instead of harping on what you don't want (Why don't you ever do Y?)

In any relationship you have to pick your battles, so try to let the small things slide and see the good instead of picking at the bad. A lot of battles are losing ones because most men don't care about the things that women do. He may not see the point in hanging his coat in the closet when there's a great spot for it over on the chair, a more convenient spot at that because he can easily grab it when he needs to go back out again. Yes, you find this incredibly annoying, but if you nag him about it then you become the annoying one. If certain things really bother you then definitely bring them up, but again, try to let the small things slide.

Being Too Critical

I don't know why we do it, but we ladies just can't seem to stop ourselves from picking our men apart. We might really love them, we might be totally turned on by them, we might think they're amazing in every way...yet we will always manage to find something wrong, something that could use just a little tweaking. I have a theory that this is a way of protecting ourselves from being hurt, a kind of defense mechanism that stops us from getting in too deep. Or maybe we just naturally see the potential in people and have a strong desire to see that potential realized.

Criticism and nagging are kind of under the same umbrella, but criticism can take a more sinister form as it attacks the person, not simply the behavior.

Usually when we're critical of other people, it's because we are critical of ourselves. Try being nicer to yourself and learning to appreciate who you are, and see how this carries over into your interactions with others. Being too critical can stir up a lot of resentment in the relationship from the one being criticized, and resentment ruins relationships, so do whatever it takes to control your critical instincts.

Not Appreciating Him

It is essential to train yourself to stop looking at the things he isn't doing and look at what he *is* doing, and then acknowledge and appreciate him for it! The more you show you appreciate him, the more he'll try to please you.

Appreciation is the number-one way to a man's heart. I've interviewed countless guys over the years as part of my research for my books and articles, and the most consistent thing I hear is how much they crave appreciation and how much of a turn-off it is when a girl acts entitled and unappreciative.

Pay attention to the nice things he does and express appreciation. Maybe you think a guy *should* pay for dates, but that doesn't mean you should expect it and not thank him for it. When I was dating I would always send a thank-you text to the guys I liked after a date, and I'd make sure it was more personalized than, "Thank you for dinner, it was great!" I really tried to consider the effort that went into whatever the night's activity was and show appreciation for that. When I started doing this I always got asked out on another date! And even today, as a married lady, I always, *always* show my husband appreciation for everything. (I believe that's the reason he's so willing to do anything for me!)

Appreciation is essential, so much so that a guy will avoid a relationship, or break off a relationship, when a woman won't or can't show him sufficient appreciation.

Being Bitter/Whiny/Grouchy

We all have bad days, and that's understandable. However, it's in your best interest to try to be happy and positive. In general, we're drawn to people who are happy and who radiate a positive energy.

There is nothing lovable about someone who is demanding, nagging, sarcastic, bitter, frustrated, or angry. That's not to say he'll stop loving you when you're like this (love doesn't turn on and off like a light switch) but it will be harder for him to act loving towards you when you're negative. Being mad at him for not spending enough time with you won't fill him with a strong desire to be around you, because no one likes being around someone who is angry and no one likes doing things because he was guilted into it.

Being fun and pleasant is what will make him want to spend time with you. When you're happy and you appreciate him and bring positive energy into your interactions, he'll become addicted to you. He'll want to clear his entire schedule for more time with you, for more of that amazing feeling, because nothing else in his life can give him that. Nothing else can compete with the feeling of being with a woman who is thoroughly happy with who he is.

Dumping Your Insecurities onto Him

It's not his fault if you feel fat or your skin is breaking out or you found a tiny wrinkle by your mouth or you're scared he'll leave you for someone shiny and new; these are *your* issues and hang-ups, so don't turn them into relationship problems.

If he's with you, it's a given that he finds you attractive. Don't talk him out of his attraction by highlighting all your flaws. Chances are he won't even notice them until you point them out, so why draw attention to them? Men are attracted to confident women, so not only will you be making him aware of your flaws, you'll be diminishing his overall attraction to you by appearing insecure.

Trying to Change Him

Don't ever, *ever* get into a relationship thinking the other person will change; this is a massive mistake. So is trying to change your partner. The amazing thing about relationships is that we often do change and evolve along the way. We become better, more sensitive, more caring. We see ourselves more clearly, both our weaknesses and our strengths. This is a natural part of being in a healthy relationship, but it doesn't come about by force; it happens naturally when we start out accepting and appreciating the other person for exactly who he is.

This will sound counterintuitive, but if you want someone to change, you need to be in a place where you totally accept him and completely love him *for exactly who he is right now.* If you can't do that, then it may be worthwhile to consider whether or not this is really a person you want to be in a relationship with.

How to Ruin a Budding Relationship

The beginning of a relationship is often the most confusing

time, a time when everything seems precarious and you don't quite know where you stand or where, if anywhere, the relationship is going.

Men and women are different and so the way they experience and process relationships is different. Men tend to be much more in the moment. If the relationship is enjoyable in the here and now, they're happy. If it's unpleasant, they either distance themselves or leave. Women, on the other hand, tend to get stuck in where the relationship is going and the "clues," both real and imagined, that will supposedly give them the answer. In the midst of this quest to figure out what's going on and where a man stands, women often lose sight of what's important (the actual relationship, and how it is in the here and now).

Here are five things you might unknowingly be doing that can ruin your relationship:

1. Jumping the Gun

This scenario might sound familiar to you. You meet a guy and instantly hit it off. You go out a few times and realize that he basically has every quality you want in a man. You don't want to do it, but you can't help but think how perfect it would be if it worked out and you ended up together. You think about all the crazy coincidences that led to your meeting him (if there weren't any, you'll find some to make this a great "how we met" story!) and feel certain that this union was written in the stars. You're not even official with him yet, but you could never conceive of dating another guy...that would almost be like having an affair! You're sure this guy is the one, you're positive of it. You have an amazing time together, you talk for hours, things are great, except…you're on two completely different pages!

What's the harm? you might wonder, *it's not like he knows you've already picked out the china pattern for your wedding registry.* Oh, but he does. They always do.

Men are not the boneheads sitcoms would have you believe. They are very much in tune with the vibe and energy a woman gives off. And when a man feels that pressure, even the slightest pressure, he will back off. When this happens, you will of course start to panic and may cling even tighter, thinking you'd be a fool to let the love of your life slip away! The more you push, the more he pulls away, until there's nothing left but the memory of him and the pain of thinking what might have been.

Due to the nature of my career, people talk to me about their relationships. A *lot*. I hear it from guys and I hear it from girls. The funny thing I've noticed is that when a girlfriend starts dating a new guy and I ask her how it's going, she'll usually say something like "It's great! I can totally see myself marrying someone like him." While when I talk to my guy friends about a new girl, they'll usually say, "She's great, I definitely want to go out with her again." So the woman is planning the wedding while the guy is planning the next date. Talk about worlds apart.

A friend of mine recently went on two dates with a guy and started talking to me about all the problems that might emerge down the line and how she'll deal with them. What if his startup idea fails? Could she be with a guy who doesn't have job stability? What if she had to be the breadwinner?

Could she respect him if he wasn't providing for the family? (The family?! They barely knew each other at this point!) She was in a total tizzy until I told her to relax and stop trying to solve relationship problems that haven't happened yet. I advised her to focus instead on deciding if she wants to go on a third date…easy-peasy!

The important thing to realize about men is that they're very in the moment. Women can be, too, but more often they can't help but get a little overzealous when a promising prospect comes along. Like I said, this sort of pressure can be a huge turn-off and can transform a promising relationship into a nonexistent one real fast. So take a breath, quiet the chatter in your mind, and focus on enjoying your relationship for what it is, as it is, right here and right now.

2. Overanalyzing

Look, I am not casting stones here. I've been writing about relationships for years and I still used to catch myself overanalyzing my relationships all the time. Overanalyzing ties into the jumping too many steps ahead because they're both essentially rooted in fear.

You meet a great guy and you can't help but feel a little worried that your feelings won't be reciprocated. In an attempt to protect yourself, you look at the "clues" in his behavior and try to figure out what everything means. If something seems like a bad sign, you focus on solving it, stat! You pick apart his texts and e-mails, you debate endlessly over what to respond and whether an emoticon would seem cheesy or cute, you spend hours talking to your friends about why he's taking so long to text back and what it means and what he might be up to. You replay every moment of every interaction with him, keeping tally of the signs he likes you and signs he doesn't. It's exhausting. I'm exhausted just thinking about it!

The truth is, 90% of relationship problems wouldn't exist if women would stop obsessing and analyzing and just go with it.

What's more, the more time you spend thinking and talking about him, the more you're investing in him and the more hurt you'll be if the relationship ends. Guys like their relationships and their lives to be simple and drama free. The most attractive woman to a guy is one who goes with the flow and can be present in the relationship without putting too much pressure on it. If you're playing "emotional detective," you'll be too busy worrying about the relationship to actually enjoy it!

The best attitude to have is one where you feel happy with your guy, but would be OK without him. Don't waste your time trying to figure out if he likes you and what he meant when he said XYZ, instead be confident and trust that he does like you, because why wouldn't he? And if for whatever reason he doesn't, who cares?! You'll find someone else who does.

3. Acting Official Before You're Actually Official

OK now, this is by far the biggest relationship-ruining mistake. Girl meets boy, girl really, *really* likes boy, girl cuts off all other potential suitors and focuses exclusively on boy even though they never decided to be exclusive. How this usually turns out is boy ends up telling girl "I like our relationship as it is and don't want to label it" and girl is devastated but stays in the relationship anyway, hoping he'll change his mind.

Look, I know it's tough to keep your options open when you find a guy who shines so much brighter than the rest, but you cannot act like his girlfriend until you are his girlfriend. Why? Because most guys are not going to willingly deepen a level of commitment unless they have to.

It's not that guys are anti-monogamy, or don't want to commit; it just isn't a man's natural inclination to want to be tied down. A man will only commit himself to a woman if he is inspired to and if it benefits him. If he's getting all the benefits of having a girlfriend without the obligations, why in the world would he change that situation?

If you don't necessarily want to date multiple guys at a time that's fine, just do not act like his girlfriend until you are. Don't take down your online dating profiles or prioritize him over everything else in your life or invest in him any further until he reciprocates.

4. Dropping Your Life for Him

This is another common relationship trap. You start seeing a guy, you spend more and more time together, and suddenly he is just about the only thing you have going on in your life. You ditch your friends for him, don't go to the gym as often, don't go to book club. The reason this guy was drawn to you in the first place was because you had a well-rounded, fulfilling life that you enjoyed. You can't expect to abandon the things that make you who you are and have him feel the same level of attraction and intrigue towards you.

When you abandon all the things that make you you, not only does it make you less attractive to him, it also creates an unspoken expectation that he is going to fill in the empty space and be the sole source of your happiness and fulfillment. That is way too much pressure for anyone! Also, if you give up your life for him and come to expect him to do the same for you, he will begin to resent you for taking away his freedom.

The point is, don't stop being who you were before the relationship after you're in it. Keep your life balanced, fun, and fulfilling, with many sources of happiness.

5. Not Seeing the Relationship for What It Is

When it comes to relationships, the devil is in the delusions. A lot of us have a truly amazing ability to see exactly what we want to see and ignore the truth in front of us.

A guy might say he doesn't want a relationship with you, but you stick around, knowing with certainty that he'll change his mind. You convince yourself that he doesn't really mean it. You are positive that he cares about you because he took you to a fancy restaurant, he said he missed you, he told you about his hopes and dreams…any nice thing he said or did from the time you met is tallied up and used as proof that he really cares. And all the stuff he did that indicates he isn't serious? Well, we can just ignore those and take a glass-half-full sort of approach!

Before entering into a relationship, you must be clear with yourself about exactly what you want. If you're not, then it's far too easy to get caught up in something you don't want. I get so many questions from women who are upset or angry at their guy for reasons that are completely invalid. For instance, he told her he doesn't want to be exclusive, she continues seeing him anyway, and then she gets mad at him when she catches him texting another girl. So she's mad at him for not acting like he's in a real relationship even though they are not in a real relationship.

Know the kind of relationship you want. It's OK to admit that you want to get married or to be in a committed relationship. I know in this day and age it's considered passé for women to admit to such things—instead we're supposed to be independent and strong and not need a man—but if that's what you want, give yourself permission to want it. The first step to getting what you want is knowing what it is.

6. Not Seeing the Guy for Who He Is

When it comes to relationships, most women have a tendency to focus on the potential of the guy they're dating more than on who he actually is at that point in time. Helping a man reach his full potential can be an incredible and beautiful thing. However, it can take a toll on you if you let this desire run wild, and that is where things get sticky.

For instance, a woman in an abusive relationship may find herself unable to leave because although she knows this isn't the kind of relationship she wants and this isn't the way she deserves to be treated, she sees the good guy the abuser could be and doesn't want to let him go, even though the person in her head doesn't even really exist.

I think we've all found ourselves in these kinds of situations, though maybe not as extreme.

A friend of mine started dating the man of her dreams a few years ago. He literally checked every box on her long list of ideal man traits. At first, everything was amazing. He was sweet and attentive and romantic. It was going so well she felt like she was starring in her very own romantic comedy, but this was real life! But then things started to change...

As things got more serious, his darker side came out. He gradually became very critical of her and his derogatory remarks and snide comments became more and more frequent. He was also struggling with his own issues; he felt depressed, he didn't like his job and wanted to change fields, and he felt dissatisfied with his life overall. She tried to help, but it only made things worse, and he started blaming her for the way he was feeling. Any time she tried to talk about it he would withdraw and go cold and shut her out completely.

Even though she felt completely alone in the relationship and no longer confident in herself due to his biting insults, she stayed as committed as ever. Not only that, she saw it all as her fault. She knew he had the ability to be great; he had been great earlier in their relationship so maybe it was her fault he'd changed.

She became completely blind to the man he actually was and focused exclusively on the man he could be. The more he retreated, the more she desperately tried to win him back—to motivate him, to inspire him, to turn him into the man she thought he was deep down. Unfortunately, her efforts were in vain. Not only didn't he change, he eventually dumped her and didn't look back. She was left crushed and broken-hearted, and it took her years to pick up the pieces. He, on the other hand, moved on without missing a beat and quickly got engaged and married to someone else. Part of the reason she had a harder time moving on was because of how much she'd invested in and given to the relationship. And the reason she'd invested so heavily was partly because of her love for him, but mostly because of her love for who she thought he was deep down and could become.

Being able to see someone else's potential is a very powerful skill that we women are blessed with. However, it has to be kept in its place. Believing in someone and helping him through difficulties is one thing. Staying in a relationship with a man who is incapable of giving you what you need and who ends up dragging you down is quite another.

This situation will make him feel like a failure for not being what you want, and it will make you feel like a failure for not succeeding in getting him to be the man you know he's capable of being.

In a relationship, you have to accept the person for who they are, exactly as they are, and you have to assume they aren't going to change.

If it's a healthy relationship where both parties are in stable places emotionally, you will naturally bring out the best in one another, including each other's hidden potential. If it's an unhealthy relationship, you will only tear each other down.

Having a bad day or a bad week is understandable, but that's not what I'm talking about. What I'm talking about is a continued pattern of unacceptable behavior.

A lot of girls trap themselves by staying in the relationship because of how great the guy used to be. They'll wait around in dead-end or toxic relationships for months or even years, sustained only by the hope that he will one day be nice and charming again.

I don't think I need to explain further why this is a terrible, and often devastating, mistake.

So ladies, celebrate the fact that we are compassionate beings who can see a man's potential. But also remember that while it's one of our greatest strengths, it can also be our greatest weakness, and we need to be mindful to use it at the right time and in the right situation.

Did Sleeping with Him Too Soon Ruin the Relationship?

A close friend of mine recently met an amazing guy on an online dating site. He was smart, successful, and a dead ringer for Bradley Cooper. Things got off to a promising start.

They exchanged a few flirty messages and he asked her to go out on a Saturday night. They had an amazing time on the date, they continued to message, and he asked her out early in the week for the following Saturday. Another nice date with pleasant conversation and mutual enjoyment of each other's company (and some passionate making out) and he again reserved her for the following Saturday night.

Before the third date she told me she was a little unsure about him. She thought he was great on paper and all, but she didn't really feel like they had too much to talk about—she mostly just thought he was really hot. She decided she was going to sleep with him after their third date, and I didn't really offer much in the way of advice since it didn't seem like she was interested in having a real relationship with him.

So they had a passionate night together and continued to text one another, but something had shifted…

My friend told me that she was waiting for him to ask her out for that Saturday night because she had purchased tickets to a booze cruise and thought that would make a fun date. He usually booked her in advance so when he still hadn't asked her out by Thursday she started to panic.

They were still in contact; he would still text her messages full of sexual

innuendoes. But sometimes he didn't text, or would just drop off when she asked him about something non-sex related.

Suddenly, their relationship went from elegant Saturday night dates to random 2 AM hookups. He never texted her earlier than 11 PM, and while he was nice and sweet when they hung out, all he wanted to do was fool around (and sometimes order in food and fool around).

I stood silently by as the whole thing started to unravel. I make it a policy not to give my friends relationship advice unless they explicitly ask for it, and in situations like this they often prefer to stay in denial land! Also, my friends sometimes get mad at me for not giving them the answers they want, so in order to keep the peace I will stay mum until things get dire.

And when they did finally get dire, my friend called me up and said: "I don't get this, I really, really like him. What did I do wrong?"

I first pointed out that she hadn't started really, *really* liking him until he stopped acting like he really liked her. But even still, I told her flat out that she'd slept with him too soon. It was a pretty open and shut case, probably one of the easiest relationship questions I'd ever gotten.

"What do you mean?" She countered. "I waited until the third date! Isn't that what you're supposed to do?"

I didn't respond immediately to her question. "OK, well tell me this. What did you actually know about this guy?"

"Ummm…well, he showed me pictures of his nieces and nephews and talked about them!"

"Doesn't count. Anyone on Facebook could see the pictures and I'm sure he talks about them to his friends and coworkers. What do you know about him that you couldn't find out from his online dating profile or Facebook page?"

Do you know what his ultimate goals are? His fears? What makes him happy? What his weak points are?"

"Well, no…"

And therein lies the problem. She slept with him before they'd developed any sort of a real connection. They were still in the "casual getting to know one another" phase. He hadn't shown any level of investment (I know going on three Saturday night dates in a row with a guy can feel like he's investing, but he's not). They didn't really know each other except for superficial details.

When it comes to sleeping with a guy, the number of dates is an arbitrary measure of the state of your relationship. What matters is the quality of the time you spend together. A girl who sleeps with a guy on the first date after an evening of intense, meaningful conversation that fosters a bond is much more likely to have a lasting relationship than a girl who sleeps with a guy on the fifth date when she hasn't really formed a connection with him.

The guy my friend was dating never really invested in her. Yes, he was attracted and somewhat interested, but after sex was in the mix he lost interest in pursuing things further. Why should he take her out on nice dates and wine and dine her when he can call her at 1am when he's feeling horny and get his needs met? When sex comes before a real emotional connection has been established, it's hard to rewind the clock.

The right time to sleep with a guy is when he's shown he's invested in you. Period. (This is assuming you want a relationship with him. If you want a friend with benefits or steady booty call, then sleep with him whenever you want, just be safe!)

This doesn't necessarily mean he calls you his girlfriend or has said he loves you. It means you both are able to drop your masks and be real when you're together. It means he shares things with you he doesn't share with other people in his life (and vice versa). It means he cares about you and respects you as a person.

As women, we've been told all our lives that we need to make a guy wait for sex, like it's some sort of carrot to dangle in front of him in order to get what we want out of him. I get where the idea comes from and there is a grain of truth in there. The fact is, men don't value what they perceive is readily and easily available to all other men.

When you sleep with a guy before you really know him, it's easy for him to assume that any other guy could have done it. When you sleep with him after getting to know who he truly is, he believes that you slept with him because of how amazing he is, and you wouldn't have chosen to sleep with just any other guy.

Guys appreciate women who are genuine and authentic, and you'd be surprised how easily a man can distinguish between a woman holding out to manipulate him into feeling what she wants him to feel, and a woman who holds out because she respects herself and is still trying to decide if this man is worth investing in any further.

Sex and relationships are two entirely different things for men; they don't necessarily see sex as a measure of the depth of the relationship the way most women do. For guys, sex is more of a reward for being in the relationship. Having sex with a guy is not enough to make him want to commit. Men do not get into relationships purely based on physical attraction, and a man wanting to sleep with you is not a measure of his actual *feelings* for you.

Before sleeping with him you have to understand that having sex with him will not guarantee a relationship or any sort of commitment. If that's what you're hoping for then you're setting yourself up to be greatly disappointed. It seems obvious yet so many women get tripped up in this area. Before sleeping with a guy you have to determine if he's interested in you or interested in having *sex with you*. The trouble is, it's not always easy to distinguish between these two vastly different things.

The right time to sleep with a guy is unique to every person and every relationship. You can't apply a three-date rule to every situation—only you know when the time is right. Sometimes it will be obvious, and other times you'll have to dig really deep to make sure you aren't deluding yourself.

If you genuinely care for him and know in your heart that he feels the same about you (and as I've said many times, when a guy likes you, it's obvious) and you want to express your feelings in a physical way, then go for it. If you are unsure of how he feels, but are afraid he'll leave you if you don't put out, then please trust your gut and make sure you're putting yourself and your needs first.

When a man truly cares about you, you'll know because he'll show he cares about you. He'll make you a priority in his life, he'll want to get to know you (the real you), he'll bring you into his world and he'll want to be brought into yours, he'll put effort into the relationship, he'll commit to you. He won't just tell you he cares, he'll show it through his actions and he'll leave little room for doubt about how he truly feels. If you don't quite know where you stand yet, then wait a little longer. This is another way to see where he stands, because a guy who truly cares about you won't mind waiting.

Just be sure not to sleep with a guy for any of the following reasons:

- **You're afraid he's going to leave or lose interest.**
  First, it says something about the dynamic of the relationship if you're having these feelings, and you should spend time pondering why you feel this way. Is it insecurity? Is he not treating you right? Does he feel confused by your decision to hold out because he thinks sex is the expected next step? Whatever the reason, don't have sex with him if you're doing it in a bid to keep him around or interested.

- **He's pressuring you.** Never ever have sex because you feel pressured. This is where personal boundaries come into play. If you aren't ready then you aren't ready. Don't apologize for it, don't make excuses for it, don't justify yourself to make him feel better. If he can't handle it, then that's his problem, not yours.

- **To deepen the relationship.** Sex will not deepen your bond or connection if it isn't there before the sex. A man will not fall in love with you because you slept with him, nor will the act make him realize that he wants to commit himself to you. Giving a man great sex will never be enough to inspire him to commit. Men commit and fall in love for reasons that are completely separate from sex.

- **To prove he likes you or to feel desired.** A man can have sex with a woman he hates as long as he's attracted to her…and even if he isn't—as they say, everyone's a supermodel in the dark. A man having sex with you does not say anything about whether or not he likes you. Does it mean he desires you? Yes. But using sex as a means for validation and to feel desired points to much deeper issues that need to be addressed. Of course, everyone likes to be wanted and desired. However, you should never sleep with a man to feel validated. When you sleep with a guy it causes the release of certain hormones like oxytocin that make you feel even more close and connected to him. If your relationship isn't established, then you might have a hard time distinguishing between intimacy in the bedroom and emotional intimacy, and this just opens the doors wide for hurt and disappointment.

With all relationship issues, the best advice is to love yourself, know your worth, and work constantly on being the best version of yourself that you can. When you place a high value on yourself, the world will follow suit. And when you value yourself enough to work on yourself, you will get to know yourself and will be more aware of your needs and desires. Ultimately you will have the strength and clarity to get what you truly want. More on this in the next chapter, so keep going!

Remember This

There are many ways to ruin a relationship and push him away, but they are all essentially caused by one thing: a lack of self-esteem. When you don't love yourself, you won't fully believe someone else can love you, and this can lead you to push love away even though it's the very thing you crave.

6

Good Relationships Start With You

The love you feel in life is a reflection of the love you feel in yourself.

– Deepak Chopra

A successful relationship essentially comes down to two things: the right person at the right time. The first thing that's important to remember when it comes to relationships is that in general, like attracts like. That is, what you are or think you are is what you will attract.

If you don't value yourself, you will go for someone who doesn't treat you well and you will be OK with it because he's just validating how you feel about yourself.

If you are emotionally unavailable, you will attract a guy who is emotionally unavailable. Now, you can want to be in a relationship and at the same time be unavailable in your own way. If you're afraid of getting hurt or feel like the guys you want always leave you, then you might subconsciously be putting up walls to protect yourself.

In order to attract a real relationship, you first need to make sure that you are in the right place emotionally. Make sure you want a relationship for the right reasons, not just to fill a void or make you feel better about yourself. You also need to develop a firm sense of who you are, and you need to learn how to be happy without a relationship.

It may seem like finding a great guy who likes you and sticks around, when others couldn't or wouldn't, will take the sting out of past rejection, but it doesn't work that way. If you're still holding onto hurt from the past, then it will spill over into your relationships in the present.

Loving Yourself and Being More Confident

Good self-esteem attracts someone capable not only of healthy interactions but of loving you for who you are. If you're not sure of yourself inside, you'll seek validation outside.

Low self-esteem can prevent you from having the kind of love you want, and if you're in a relationship it can wreck the love you have. A romantic partner can certainly make you feel good, but they can never be the sole source of your self-esteem. If you don't already feel good about yourself, none of his compliments or caresses or demonstrations of love will have an impact, and you won't really be able to trust that he's genuine. It makes sense on a rational level, because how can you ever accept that someone else loves you if you don't already love yourself? If not even you think you're lovable then how could anyone else?

The fact is, you can only let in as much love from the outside as you feel on the inside. If you don't feel good about yourself, you will never truly believe that someone else can love you. You will constantly be on the lookout for the other shoe to drop, for the guy you care about to leave, thus validating the "fact" that you are unworthy of love.

Self-esteem has significant, far-reaching ramifications for all areas of our lives. Building your sense of confidence and self-worth isn't always easy, but it can dramatically change your life for the better. Here are some tips to get there:

Stop Thinking Negative Thoughts

Negative thoughts are inevitable. Sometimes we think them to ourselves and other times we lament out loud in hopes of getting some reassurance: "I'm so Fat." "I'm so Gross." "I'm never going to be successful." You know how the good old insecurity song and dance goes. Well from now on, stop entertaining these thoughts! When a negative thought pops into your head, cut it off right then and there. A technique I like to use is to think the exact opposite when a bad thought enters my mind. If I start thinking, "Ugh, I'm so tired, I so do not *want* do any work today," I'll identify that this is a negative thought of no value to me and then say the exact opposite, "I am so energized! I'm going to get so much done today!" It may sound silly, but trust me, it works.

Thoughts are real forces, and they have a huge impact on your mood and mindset. When you're thinking negative thoughts, you are creating a self-fulfilling prophecy. The good news is that you can control the thoughts that enter your mind, and you don't have to pay attention to the negative ones. Every thought resonates through your mind and body and creates a vibration, which will make those thoughts a reality. If you don't want to have a bad day or feel bad about yourself, then start thinking great thoughts!

Figure Out What Confidence Looks Like

It doesn't matter what other people think of you, it's the thoughts you have about yourself that make all the difference. If you want to be more confident, then make a list that details what confidence looks like and act accordingly. If you want to try out a bold look but feel hesitant, tell yourself: "'A confident person doesn't care what other people think, and I'm a confident person and I like this outfit so I'll wear it!"

If you're afraid of approaching a guy because you're scared he'll reject you, say to yourself, "A confident person doesn't fear rejection because a confident person knows she's fabulous and a catch in every sense, and whoever doesn't see that is missing out. I am a confident person and I will be satisfied if this guy responds well to me, but it won't affect me if he doesn't." If a guy is taking forever to text back and you start to panic, tell yourself: "A confident person doesn't stress over whether a guy will text back, she assumes he will, because why wouldn't he? She doesn't really care if he never resurfaces because if he doesn't, that's his loss." You get the idea. It may feel weird, or maybe like you're being delusional, but trust me, in time you will no longer be acting like a confident person, you will be one.

Find Your Own Happiness

Having a significant other is a wonderful thing, but it isn't the only thing and it certainly doesn't make you complete or give you happiness. If you don't have a special someone in your life, that's OK. It can actually be great because you get to be totally selfish and live life only for you, a luxury people in couples do not enjoy!

Before you can be happy with someone else, you truly need to find happiness within yourself. We are all wonderful, amazing creatures, and given that we certainly do not need a man to mirror this right back to us.

Happiness doesn't just happen, it's a choice you make and something you have to work on every day. It's far too easy to get caught up in everything that's wrong in your life, and it takes a bit of practice to train yourself to look at what's going right.

Negative thoughts seldom come one at a time. The minute you start focusing on one thing that's going wrong, all you'll see is everything that's wrong. And if you're one of the many women who think she'll be happy as soon as she's in a relationship...stop! Relationships do not lead to happiness and being single does not lead to a life of misery. The right relationship can certainly enhance your overall feelings of happiness, but it can never fill a void for you. Happiness always comes from within.

Put your focus on activities that make you happy rather than on finding a relationship. Living a balanced, meaningful life will make you a more desirable person, and you'll be more likely to meet someone special.

Stay Connected to Your Essence

We all have that one thing that makes us feel alive, that thing that makes us connected to our core. For me it's writing. Even though sometimes it's a struggle to put pen to paper, when I get in that zone there is nothing like it. I feel laser-focused and all my other needs melt away. On days when I really dedicate myself to writing and produce a lot, I feel amazing. I feel on top of the world. I feel energized and inspired and charged up, and that carries over into the rest of my day and makes me more productive in all areas. I'm also happier and in a better mood.

I know people who feel the same way when they paint or draw or dance or sing or exercise or cook or travel or go to museums or give advice. We all have that one thing that gives us a sense of accomplishment, a sense of purpose. Whatever that is for you, go after it. It won't always be easy, there will be times when you're too stressed or tired or busy. But make an effort to make the time, even if it's only for ten minutes a day.

Try This Self-Love Exercise

Most people can't just know something intellectually; we need to feel it emotionally to really *know it*. This is why so many people have a hard time giving up smoking. Intellectually we all know the risks. (And if you were unaware, it says it right there on the box: smoking kills!) Telling smokers the facts doesn't usually have an impact; you have to get to the emotional core of why they smoke.

Now in relationships, why would you need your partner

to keep telling you he loves you? This knowledge was established the first time he said it. It's not like the people in a couple are learning something new every time the other person says, "I love you."

Imagine if after your boyfriend told you he loves you for the first time he said, "OK, glad we established that. I'll be sure to let you know if anything changes." I don't think you'd be too thrilled because the reason you want him to keep saying the words is not to know it, it's to *feel it.*

Every time he says it, you feel it. The reason you feel it is because you associate those words with all the things he's done to make you feel loved throughout the course of the relationship.

In order to really know anything, you have to feel it. This is true of just about everything in life.

When it comes to developing confidence and self-love, telling yourself over and over "I have self-love" won't work, and neither will keeping a running tab of your attributes or blowing kisses to yourself in the mirror.

Sure it's nice to be aware of all the wonderful things that make you, you, but telling yourself "I'm smart, I'm beautiful, I'm caring, I'm fun" isn't enough to firmly ingrain these beliefs into your psyche.

And if you aren't firm in these convictions, you become susceptible to questioning yourself when something happens that doesn't align with these notions (not getting attention from men, your boyfriend acting flaky, someone undermining you, etc.)

To experience feeling whole and complete, you need to feel the things that you already know.

A while back I learned this exercise from a teacher who has done extensive work in the field of psychology, and I put my own spin on it. A lot of my readers gave it a try and experienced amazing, almost life-changing results. So here it is:

Take a piece of paper and write Self-Love in the middle. Then around it write down 5-10 instances when you experienced love.

They can be times when you did something kind for someone else, moments when you felt proud of yourself, times when you felt completely content and secure with yourself or any time that you gave or received love.

You can also jot down quotes about love that strike a chord with you (you'll find a million of them on the A New Mode Facebook and Instagram pages if you need ideas!) or times when you witnessed selfless love in its purest form.

Once you have a list, meditate on these memories. Close your eyes and allow your mind to reflect on each memory. Paint a picture of the scene; see yourself and how you felt in that moment. If it's a quote or song lyric, reflect on the meaning of the words and try to paint a picture of what that idea would look like.

The second your mind starts to wander, think about the next example. Keep going until you've experienced all of them (take about 5-10 minutes to do this).

The mind is a tricky thing because it doesn't want to focus on a single topic for more than a few seconds. By creating images and letting your mind move from one instance to the next, you will maintain an unbreakable concentration.

As you go deeper, you will actually feel the positive emotions. When done right, this exercise is incredibly powerful and transformative.

In general, nothing anyone says or does actually has the power to affect your mood and your opinion of yourself unless you let it. If you're unsure of yourself, you'll be a lot more likely to allow the negativity to penetrate.

When you form the foundation of self-love, however, nothing on the outside can get you down.

When you know and feel with every fiber of your being how incredible you truly are, you will never again be at the mercy of someone else.

If your significant other acts in a way you don't understand or appreciate, you won't fall into despair. You'll realize that his actions have nothing to do with you and are no reflection of your inherent value and worth.

Why Confidence Matters in a Relationship

Now that we've discussed ways to increase your self-confidence, let's look at why it matters and how it makes a difference in your relationship. Healthy self-esteem is a prerequisite for healthy relationships. From my personal experiences and my years spent writing about relationships, I've learned that poor self-esteem is the number one cause of unhealthy relationships and the top relationship killer.

Self-esteem isn't an essential need like food or water, but it's a supplement that can either dramatically improve your life or keep you stunted and unfulfilled.

Poor self-worth is what sabotages new relationships, traps

us in bad relationships, and causes us to feel so devastated and broken when a relationship ends.

Having high self-esteem doesn't guarantee a happy relationship, but it does equip you with the skills to identify what you want and realize you deserve to get it, and the strength to walk away if something falls short. Here are ten things people with high self-esteem do differently in their relationships:

1. Confident Women Don't Analyze Whether or Not a Guy Likes Them—They Assume He Does

People with high self-esteem believe they are worthy of love and don't question how someone feels about them. They know that they are good, competent, and lovable, and trust that the right person for them will see this. They don't attach their worth to what a guy thinks, and as a result they don't feel stressed and anxious when a guy's feelings are unclear. Instead, they assume he likes them and they're able to be present in the relationship and enjoy it without being weighed down by fears and doubts.

2. Confident Women Realize That When a Relationship Falls Apart It's Because It Wasn't Right, Not Because They Did Something Wrong

Not everyone is a match; sometimes two people are just incompatible and this doesn't make either of them flawed or bad. Confident women don't take it personally when a guy doesn't want a romantic relationship. They realize that it must not be the right match and they move on with their sense of self firmly intact.

But when a girl is insecure and a guy leaves, she spirals. She may obsess, analyze, and replay every interaction in an attempt to uncover what she did wrong. She may know on a conscious level that it simply wasn't a match, but deep down she holds on to the destructive belief that she was the problem...she was unlovable and this guy and all other guys she wants will never want her back.

3. Confident Women Set Healthy Boundaries

Healthy personal boundaries and high self-esteem go hand in hand. Having strong boundaries means you prioritize your needs and your emotions and do not assume responsibility for someone else's needs and emotions.

Confident women know what they will and will not accept and don't allow themselves to be pressured or guilted into doing things they don't want to do. They act in accordance with who they are and what they believe and don't tailor their behavior for a guy, or do things solely to keep him interested and happy. When you have weak boundaries, you may sell yourself out in a relationship and put up with treatment that you know objectively is unacceptable.

A woman with healthy boundaries will not lose herself in a relationship and will not allow her identity to be contingent upon how a man sees her. She will continue to maintain her own life outside of the relationship without giving up her friends, hobbies, or alone time. She won't abandon important parts of herself or her life for the sake of the relationship. She brings her fully formed self into the relationship, and if the guy wants something else, or something more that she doesn't have to offer, she will leave.

4. Confident Women Trust Themselves and the Decisions They Make

A key component of having high self-esteem is trusting yourself to make the right choices while also realizing you are well equipped to cope should things go awry. People with high self-esteem don't constantly question their actions or feel conflicted about the right thing to say or do. They act on how they feel and are comfortable being their true, authentic selves.

People with low self-esteem don't trust their judgment, don't trust their gut instincts, and are afraid of being wrong. As a result, they either live their lives in a constant state of anxiety or they depend completely on others to guide them along the right path. This obviously does not do much to help one's sense of autonomy, which is also a key element of healthy self-esteem.

5. Confident Women Don't Show off or Talk Themselves Up

Confident people don't need to tell the world how great they are. Only insecure people secretly feel that they are unworthy and feel the need to hide this by bragging about their achievements or talking themselves up.

A woman who reveals herself gradually, carefully peeling back layers of herself over time, is significantly more attractive than a woman who lays it all out there. When you feel that you are worthy, you don't need to tell people...they just know. A big mistake insecure women make in the early stages of dating is trying to sell themselves to a guy. This can be completely innocent, but it comes from a deeper sense of insecurity and inadequacy. Confident women don't need to sell themselves; rather, they use dating as a means to determine which guys are worthy of their time and affection.

6. Confident Women Accept Responsibility

Confident people accept responsibility for their actions and emotions. They don't blame or shame their partners if they feel unhappy and don't accuse him of "making" them feel a certain way. They don't blame men for being jerks and they don't view themselves as the victims of other people and circumstances.

They realize that their time is their responsibility. As a result, they don't wait around in dead-end relationships, hoping something will magically change, and they don't blame their exes for wasting their time. They take responsibility for their choices, both good and bad, and use mistakes as opportunities to grow and become even better.

7. Confident Women Take the Relationship for What It Is and Don't Need It to Be a Certain Way

Confident people feel secure in their relationships. They don't need to have a title or a ring as some sort of confirmation that the guy cares. They are able to just be present and in the relationship and let it unfold organically, without force or pressure. This is not to say they stay with guys who won't commit and are all cool and go-with-the-flow about it. If a guy can't commit in the way they want, then they'll move on. They are able to give and receive freely in their relationships and as a result, they don't stress out about labels. They just know that if it's right, it will work out. And if it's not right, they'll move on.

8. Confident Women Don't Stay in Bad Relationships

Confident people do not stay in relationships where they don't feel respected, appreciated, and valued. And they don't assume all the blame if a relationship isn't working and take it upon themselves to try to solve the problem by giving and doing more. They aren't afraid to walk away, and the thought that they won't be able to find something better or that they will wind up alone doesn't cross their minds. They can quickly see when a situation is damaging and will remove themselves immediately.

Only insecure people put up with treatment that is unacceptable, in large part because they feel on some level that that's what they deserve. When you learn to value yourself, you will weed out anyone who doesn't truly value you.

9. Confident Women Don't Desperately Seek Reassurance

People with high self-esteem know they are loved and lovable. They don't need a guy to remind them every day – it's just something they feel and know. When you are insecure you need constant validation and will become resentful if your partner doesn't give it to you. You'll blame him for "making you" feel insecure or unloved in the relationship. You may work harder to try to please him and earn his love, or you may withhold your love and affection to even the score. This insecurity manifests as neediness: you need constant reassurance, and if you don't get it you lash out and blame your partner for not providing it.

The fact is, if you don't feel good about yourself, nothing he does will ever be enough. If you don't truly believe you're worthy of love, you will never believe someone can love you. What happens is the relationship becomes a battle of wills: you fight for validation, he retreats because he feels pressured and suffocated, you view his retreat as a sign he doesn't love you and you fall into despair, he resents that nothing he does is good enough and resents the fact that you don't trust how he feels and so he stops trying, you see this as further proof he doesn't care…and either the relationship ends or continues to make you both miserable indefinitely.

10. Confident Women Choose Wisely

Confident people use their head and heart when choosing a romantic partner. They are able to quickly assess if someone is emotionally healthy and can give them what they need in a relationship. They don't let their ego get too intertwined with their emotions and they make sure they are fundamentally compatible with someone before they get too involved.

A core concept to understand when it comes to relationships is like attracts like. A confident person will attract another confident person. An insecure person will unconsciously seek out relationships with men who are insecure and who will make them feel more insecure. They will want the unavailable guys, the guys who can't commit, the guys who have walls up. These are the ones they will feel infatuated by, not the ones who show real, genuine interest. Oftentimes this happens because on an unconscious level, the insecure girl feels that if she can break through his walls, or get him to change his ways, then she'll really be worthy and valuable. This never, ever works. Instead, she just ends up compromising her integrity even further by chasing the relationship.

If you don't value yourself, then you will always be attracted to people who don't value you either. Confident people value and accept themselves for who they are. They embrace the good and are accepting of the not so good. As a result, they attract quality partners and are able to connect on a real, genuine level, one that leads to true intimacy and a healthy relationship.

Why Does the Woman Have to Change to Make a Relationship Work?

By now, you might be thinking, why is it always the woman's fault? Why do I have to do all this work to have a loving relationship?

Over the years many readers have said things along the lines of:

"Why can't he just accept me as I am? Why do I have to change?"

"Why don't you guys tell this stuff to men?"

"Why do I need to change anything? He should be the one to change!"

"It's not fair, he acts like a jerk and I have to be the one to work on myself?"

The easiest answer to these questions is: you are the only person you have complete control over.

You can try forcing your man to change, but I guarantee it won't work. Instead you will most likely find yourself alone.

The truth is, the way you act has a major impact over the way the other person responds. As a result, learning how to modify your behavior can lead to a much better, much happier, much more fulfilling relationship…and isn't that the ultimate goal here? And it goes without saying that you already chose a good, stable, emotionally healthy guy, as we discussed in the first chapter.

The point is not to place blame, but to take responsibility for what we bring into our interactions, whether in romantic relationships, friendships, work relationships, or with family.

I focus a lot on the importance of changing your mindset—which, in turn, changes your behavior—because these things can ultimately change your life and your relationships for the better…as long as you can see the bigger picture without getting frustrated by the effort you will need to exert.

The way you think affects not only you and your self-esteem, it can have a big impact on the people around you.

Just look at your own life for proof. When you're in a good place, things typically will go your way.

When you're in a bad place, things often go from bad to worse—you get into arguments with your friends, you're distracted at school or work and miss important deadlines, you yell at your boyfriend for something stupid, you stub your toe on a very heavy door.

When we have complaints, we usually don't realize how we might be causing the problems ourselves. It starts by looking deep within yourself and figuring out what place you're coming from.

When you come from a place of ego/insecurity/fear, it can cause another person to feel attacked, and when people feel attacked they will immediately go on the defensive.

For instance, if you complain to your boyfriend that he's never there for you or that he's acting cold or distant, he will be put on the defensive. He will perceive that you don't appreciate him and will act even more distant. Also, if he feels like you're blaming or attacking him, it will block him from being the great boyfriend that he can be.

When you're in a good place, you will be better able to speak with thoughtfulness and compassion. This will usually awaken the same value system in others, and they will be more likely to give you what you want.

We all have egos to protect. When you criticize harshly, it rarely inspires people to be better. It just puts them on the defensive and makes them inclined to point out your faults, too.

The good news is we all have an innate desire to be our best selves. When you can come from a place of confidence, understanding, and just the right amount of compassion, you will inspire the other person to bring his best self to the table, too, the side that wants to do good and reach its ultimate potential.

Becoming aware of your own sensitivities can make you

aware of what a gift it is to inspire someone to be his best self, rather than trying to force it to happen through criticism.

What does this look like in relationships? It comes down to recognizing and appreciating the other person for who he is and not placing demands on him that stem from your own insecurities.

It entails being in a good place emotionally, because when you bring your best to a relationship, most relationship problems solve themselves.

The worst thing you can do when you're unhappy in your relationship is blame the other person for *making* you feel a certain way. It may be the easier option, but it certainly isn't the most effective.

If there are problems, the best thing you can do is look within yourself and see how you can be better, both in the relationship and overall. If you're bringing your best to the table but problems persist, then it might be time to assess whether this is a relationship you want to continue.

Again, I'm not saying your boyfriend or husband should sit back while you do all the work. Both people need to put in effort to be their best selves so that they can have the best possible relationship. The reason I'm directing my advice to you, not him, is because, well, you're the one reading this book!

Finding Your Own Happiness

I've already mentioned this several times, but it bears repeating: your happiness is essential, both to your overall well-being and to your love life. Happiness and self-esteem go hand in hand, so finding ways to live a happier life will increase your sense of self-worth.

One big mistake a lot of people make in relationships is expecting the other person to make them happy. It doesn't work that way. Happiness isn't something you get from a relationship (although a relationship can certainly add to your level of happiness), it's something that spills into your relationship.

In order to find true happiness in life, you need to work on yourself and make a few adjustments to the way you live your life. These tweaks are actually pretty simple and if you do them right, you will attain the kind of genuine happiness most people spend their whole lives pursuing.

Here are 10 tips to find true happiness:

1. Don't Rely on Other People to Make you Happy

Relying on other people to make you happy will leave you endlessly disappointed. The reason most people feel unhappy in their lives is they expect other people to give them things that they can only give themselves. Think about it—if you continually outsource the task of filling a void inside of you and finding happiness, you will never be fully satisfied; instead you'll be at the mercy of everyone you meet.

Only you can control how happy you are and how you feel about yourself. Stop blaming other people for "making" you feel a certain way. Put yourself in the driver's seat and accept responsibility for your own happiness and your own sense of self-worth.

2. Conquer the Green Monster

Jealousy is one of the most destructive qualities a person can possess. In life you will inevitably come across people who are better looking, more successful, funnier, richer, etc., but who cares? I'm sure you have qualities that they're lacking. No good can ever come from envying what someone else has; it will just make you bitter and jaded.

3. Be Genuinely Happy for Other People

This is the opposite of being jealous. If people you know come upon some good fortune—an amazing job, an incredible guy, a huge raise—be happy for them. They didn't take anything away from you, and they probably struggled just like most people do on the quest to get what they want. If you put in the work, you'll reap the same reward eventually. Remember, blowing out someone else's candle will not make yours burn brighter.

4. Be Nice to People

You know who's mean? Unhappy people, that's who. Happy people feel good about themselves and about life and want to make other people feel good as well. Doing acts of kindness actually causes a chemical reaction that makes you feel really good. You can do little things, like smiling at strangers or giving up your seat on the subway for an old lady, or big things like volunteer work. For extra credit, try not to talk negatively behind someone's back, or gossip. While it may seem fun, no one ever really feels good about bashing someone else.

5. Be Grateful

There's a saying that goes: happiness isn't having what you want, but wanting what you have. Most of us are trained to look at what's wrong in our lives rather than what's right. We yearn for a better job, a better relationship, better friends, a better body—we zero in on what's missing and overlook what's right there in front of us. Try to change your filter system and instead zoom in on things to be grateful for.

6. Accept That Which You Cannot Change

There are certain things you can't change. You can't change your upbringing, your height, your general appearance. You also can't change the past. All you can do is move forward and try not to repeat the same mistakes. Don't waste your energy thinking about what a crappy lot in life you got. Instead, focus on what you have and on how you can develop qualities that will allow you to reach your full potential.

7. Do Something about That Which You Can Change

If you need to lose weight, hate your friends, are miserable at your job...do something about it! The surest way to feel good about yourself is to push yourself to go beyond what you thought you were capable of. Change isn't easy, but you only live once and no one is going to live your life for you. It's up to you to find the strength and motivation to take the steps to get what you want.

8. Let Go of Grudges

There's a saying that goes: "Holding a grudge is letting someone live in your head rent free." When you hold grudges, you're only hurting yourself. You're allowing negativity to course through you, and you're keeping yourself stuck in a painful past. Forgive the people who have wronged you and just let it go. Maybe you think they don't deserve forgiveness. Fair enough. But trust me, harboring feelings of anger and resentment is punishing you more than it's punishing them, so what's the point?

9. Let the Chips Fall Where They May

It took me a long time to realize that the sky wouldn't fall if I personally wasn't holding it up, and it's a lesson that has changed my life! Most people can't enjoy their lives because they're so busy micromanaging every detail. Yes, there is a time to make things happen. There is also a time to just let things happen. Take a breath, loosen up your grip on life, and try to adopt a bit of a laissez-faire attitude.

10. Watch the Company You Keep

Oprah once said "Surround yourself only with people who

will lift you higher," and this is a mantra I stand by. The people in your life will inevitably have an impact on you. When it comes to friends, quality is always better than quantity. Weed out the negative people in your life who drag you down, and spend more time with positive, optimistic people who see the good in you and encourage you to be your best self.

Remember This

You have a lot more power over your life than you realize. A good, loving, healthy, happy relationship starts with you, and the better place you're in emotionally, the better your relationship (and life) will be. So do whatever you need to do to get there!

7

How to Be Good at Relationships

Love is the condition in which the happiness of another person is essential to your own.

– Robert Heinlein

I know it may not seem this way, but relationships are actually surprisingly simple. A lot of women approach romantic relationships like a game of chess. They plot and strategize and worry that one wrong move will ruin everything and cost them the game. But you don't need to follow a stringent playbook to get the guy or keep him. You don't need to become someone you're not, or act in a way that isn't true to who you are.

What it really comes down to is becoming your best self while also developing an awareness and understanding of what it takes to have an amazing, loving, mutually fulfilling relationship. What it actually takes, not the idealized fantasy that so many have come to view as a reality.

Four Basic Rules to Getting the Love You Never Thought You Could Have

If you can master a few basic principles about relationships and what it takes to have the *right* relationship, you will overcome confusion and heartbreak and effortlessly get the relationship you've always wanted.

Whether you're involved or single as can be, here are the top four rules to live by to get the love you want:

1. Never Want Someone Who Doesn't Want You

Sounds obvious, but sadly, it's not! When it comes to men and relationships, we can delude ourselves in some pretty impressive ways. We find signs to prove that things are the way we want them to be and that he feels the way we want him to feel.

Now here's the truth of the matter. If a guy says or indicates he wants to be with you, but isn't actually *with you* for whatever reason (I don't like labels, my ex-girlfriend was evil, I'm stressed about my job, my dog died etc. etc.), then don't waste your time. Don't help his case by reasoning and rationalizing why his excuses make sense (but he is *really* busy! And his last girlfriend sounds like such a bitch, and his dog was his *best friend*).

When someone is giving you excuses for why he can't do something, what he's really doing is telling you he doesn't *want* to do it. Some reasons may be quite impressive and there may even be sprinkles of truth mixed in there, but when it comes down to it, if he wants to be with you, he will be. Are there exceptions? Yes, but they are very, very rare. And even if a guy can't commit for whatever reason, he will still make sure to let you know he's invested in a real and substantial way.

If a guy isn't showing you that he is committed and that he wants to be with you and only you, then stop wanting that from him. It isn't easy, but it's a far better alternative than wasting months or even years of your life waiting around for some guy to get his act together, wouldn't you agree?

2. Choose Someone Who Brings out the Best in You

Being in a relationship shouldn't be your end goal, the end goal should be attaining the *right* relationship.

When two people are in a relationship, they should bring out the best in one another. They should challenge each other to grow so that their best attributes strengthen and they become the best versions of themselves.

When a relationship crushes you and leaves you feeling paranoid, anxious, insecure, inadequate, and always on edge, just waiting for the other shoe to drop…you're cheating yourself out of having the immense benefits a good relationship can provide.

It breaks my heart seeing some of the questions I receive via email and in the forum on A New Mode. So many of our readers feel miserable and trapped by their relationships. Yet despite these agonizing feelings of hurt/despair/insecurity/fear, they are unable to extricate themselves from the situation because of their all-consuming feelings for the other person.

They get so caught up in their feelings for him, or his presumed feelings for them, that they miss the most important variable in the equation. And that is: do I like myself when I'm with this person?

I've been in relationships where I almost didn't recognize myself, ones where my flaws were magnified and my good attributes were tucked away somewhere beyond reach. It's a miserable feeling, one that can have lasting ramifications long after the relationship (inevitably) ends.

At the end of the day, you are all you have. You need to be your greatest ally in the world. You need to do what's best for you and what will make you happy and help you reach your potential. If your relationship is sending you in the opposite direction, stop wasting your strength and energy on making it work and instead use that energy to walk away.

3. Take the Word "Should" out of Your Vocabulary

If you're going to do anything, it should be to take the word should out of your vocabulary! OK, in all seriousness, the word should is very poisonous when it comes to relationships ("Always" and "Never" are tied for second). When you tell a guy what he *should* be doing, you're saying that what he is doing isn't enough.

Guys want to make you happy, seriously. Guys also need to feel like winners in the world. If you "should" him, you're basically telling him he's a loser who can't make you happy, and this will not encourage him to try any harder.

Should is a punishing word. It causes resentment to brew and it immediately places the person you're "shoulding" on the defensive. Just think about all the times someone told you what you "should" do. That word is never received pleasantly.

Instead of focusing on what your partner *should* be doing, try to look at what he is doing right in the relationship and show appreciation for those things. The more your man feels appreciated, the more he'll want to do to make you happy.

When you can come from this place, you and he will be true partners instead of adversaries and things will feel much more relaxed and effortless.

4. Be the Prize

The most common trap women fall into in relationships is trying to be good enough for the guy. They get stuck plotting and planning their every move in an effort to prove their worth to him. This is the *worst* way to be in a relationship. For one, it reeks of insecurity and neediness. It also puts the guy in the driver's seat and essentially tells him he can dictate the terms of the relationship. When this happens, you'll find yourself in a situation with a guy who will essentially do whatever he wants because he knows he can get away with it and you'll still be there.

Being the prize isn't so much a set of behaviors as it is a state of mind. The "prize" mentality is one that asks: Is *he* good enough for *me*? Of all the guys I could have, is he the one I choose? The opposite of this is thinking, "He's out of my league, I really hope he doesn't lose interest. What can I do to win him over?"

Guys want to be with a quality woman they had to work for and *earn*. There is nothing interesting or exciting about a woman who will bend over backwards and settle for scraps just because she doesn't want to be alone.

If you catch yourself obsessing over what to say to your guy, or how to act around him, stop and tell yourself: "I am the prize that *he* needs to win over."

Becoming a thoroughly confident woman takes work and isn't something that just happens. However, one route to take to get you there is to act like you're confident. As the saying goes, fake it 'til you make it!

What about Playing Games and the Chase?

By now we know that having an amazing relationship essentially comes down to being your most amazing version of you. (And choosing wisely, of course!) But you may be wondering about the chase…haven't we always been told it's essential? I get asked about it constantly because it's something that has been so firmly drummed into our minds.

Women who are good at the chase aren't necessarily good at relationships; they're just good at getting guys to chase them. I know this all too well because I used to be one of those girls, I could hook 'em and reel 'em in, but I couldn't quite keep them. Learning how to be good at relationships goes far beyond learning how to get guys to pursue you. (Although this is important to a degree, as you'll see.)

So what's the deal? Do you need to play games to get the guy?

I have a friend I jokingly refer to as my biggest muse

because this girl simply refuses to learn her lesson when it comes to men and relationships.

I try and I try to break things down for her, but she continues to make the same mistakes. While it provides me with tons of stories to use as illustrations of what *not* to do, I really wish she would take my advice a little more seriously. But if she won't, hopefully you will.

So here's the latest installment of the drama in her love life. She was dating a guy for a year who refused to call her his girlfriend, giving her some song and dance about not liking labels and having commitment issues yada yada yada.

After endless urging from me, she finally put her foot down and said she didn't want to be in this relationship no-man's-land anymore and wanted a commitment.

It's very difficult to break a relationship pattern that is firmly established (in this case he had enjoyed the benefits of having a girlfriend without the responsibility of being in a relationship for over a year), and she knew that the chances of him doing a total turnaround on the spot were slim. But she was also sick of not being "enough" for him and knew something had to be done.

The conversation went pretty much as I predicted: he still refused to commit and they ultimately decided to take a "break."

Against my advisement, she texted him several times during this break. While he would respond, his responses were pretty short and vague. I finally had to get a little harsher with her and tell her how desperate she was making herself look by constantly reaching out. I begged her to stop and let him come to her.

After a few weeks, she called me up and excitedly said, "Sabs! You were right. I haven't reached out to him in weeks and now he's begging to see me!"

While she interpreted this as a victory, I knew it was only step one in the process of getting him back and getting him to commit.

Even though I advised her to wait a week (after everything he put her through, he deserved to sweat it out), she was too excited over finally having the (perceived) upper hand and made a date with him for the following night.

They grabbed a few drinks, spent hours catching up, had a steamy make-out session...and then she came to me asking what happens next.

I gave her an exact game plan. I told her not to engage when he texts, to keep things friendly but not get overzealous. I suggested not hanging out again right away and instead pushing it off for another week, not answering his calls or messages right away and instead waiting a few hours, or even a day.

Her response was one many women have when you tell them what to do to get the guy: "But why do I have to play all these games? Why can't I just be who I am! It's ridiculous to have to strategize every single move I make."

Yes, this is true. Game playing can seem immature or even silly. It's not that you need to play games to get the guy, it's that you need to be a certain kind of girl. If you aren't that kind of girl, fake it until you make it.

If a girl is confident, loves her life, and respects herself, she will never need to play a single game. She won't pretend she doesn't have time for a guy who doesn't prioritize her; she will inherently busy herself with other things and move past him.

She won't be obsessed with trying to win over some guy who doesn't treat her right to begin with, she will skeptically give him another shot (and only if he proves himself deserving of it) and then will assess him to decide if he's worth her time.

She won't all of a sudden see a guy as soon as he decides he wants to see her. She will realize she has the power to choose and will not reduce herself to the role of waiting to be chosen.

She sees the bigger picture and isn't ruled by what she wants in the present moment.

For instance, even though she may really want a guy and truly care for him, she realizes that giving in and accepting less than what she needs won't get her what she wants in the end (a committed relationship). It would only give her the temporary satisfaction of being with him in the moment while giving way to more confusion and doubts the next day.

She can hold herself back without being afraid that the guy will move on because she isn't worth pursuing.

Whenever I would tell my friend to hold back and not respond, she would usually say "But what if he never comes back?" And she would say it with such fear in her voice, like it was the worst possible outcome she could imagine. She didn't believe she was worth fighting for. Sadly, this is a faulty mindset a lot of us may unknowingly have.

Self-fulfilling prophecies are real and powerful. If you don't believe you're worthy, you won't be. I mean, how can you expect others to believe something about you that you don't even believe about yourself? The truth is, a lot of women lack confidence and strength, and it's not something that can be gained overnight.

It takes time and it takes work. In the meantime, you have

to act as if you are the person you want to be. And this is where "games" come in.

Ideally, acting like a confident, secure woman will turn you into one.

It's not about playing games and manipulating a situation to get the outcome you want. The fact is, guys want a confident, independent woman. They want to feel *chosen* by a woman they had to *earn*.

No man will feel this way with a girl who is waiting in the wings, hoping and praying he decides she's good enough for him. If he's going to get into gear and want to commit, he needs to have a *fear of loss*.

He needs to see that you have a busy life and won't always prioritize him at the top of the list. This will make him work harder to get your time and attention.

Here is how human beings operate (this goes for all areas of life, not just relationships). When we work for something, we come to appreciate its value and will invest in it more. The more we invest in something the more we come to care about it, and the more we care about it the harder we'll work to hold onto it.

A man will only commit to you and come to care for you deeply if he has to earn you. He's not doing any work if you're waiting by the phone and willing to see him whenever he wants. And he will never truly value you if you see him as the prize that you need to win over.

A different friend of mine recently met a great guy at a party. He called her two days later asking her out, and she came to me in a panic the minute they got off the phone, say-ing: "What do I do? How should I act on the date? Are there any rules I'm supposed to be following? I really like him and I don't want to mess this up!"

This is the absolute *worst* mindset to have before a date. In this scenario, she's making him the prize that she needs to win over. She's worried about saying or doing something to turn him off and cause him to realize what she already believes to be true…that she's not good enough.

I know it's easier said than done, but you have to turn the tables and see yourself as the catch, as the one with the power to choose. If you can genuinely come from this place, you'll never have to strategize in a relationship.

Ideally you should be so happy with yourself and so confident that you will get the relationship you want and deserve that you won't settle for anything that falls short. If you're not there yet, then ignore a few calls, cancel a few dates, and follow the "rules" until you're in a place where all of this comes naturally to you.

A funny thing about "games" is that they can help you improve your confidence by finally putting you in a position of power in your relationship. When you're more confident, it will show in the decisions you make and the way you carry yourself. This will lead to even more confidence and better decision-making.

The Truth about "Good" Relationships

A lot of us have grand ideas about what a "good relationship" with the "right man" looks like. If you're single, you use this vision as fuel to keep you going through the lonely nights and bad dates, telling yourself that one day all the pain will be worth it. You believe there is a light at the end of the tunnel, a man who will be everything you've ever wanted and make you happier than you ever thought possible. If you're in a relationship, you question if you should stay when things get rocky or problems arise. These doubts make you wonder if he really is the man for you, because aren't you supposed to "just know" when the right one comes along? And if that is the case, then are these moments of uncertainty a sign that it's not right?

It's no secret that our society idealizes love. Starting in early childhood we get inundated with idealized portrayals of eternal love, from Disney movies to Nicholas Sparks novels. We develop expectations of what love should be, how it should feel, what it should look like…and we feel disappointed when reality doesn't quite align with those expectations.

Here's the thing that no one really tells you: good relationships don't always *feel* all that good…but it's not for the same reason bad relationships feel bad.

Bad relationships are the ones filled with drama. The highs are higher and the lows are lower. When I say "bad relationship," I mean everything from a toxic, codependent situation to a relationship with a man who won't commit in a significant way, to a match that is simply incompatible.

These "bad relationships" are a great escape from real life. They give you the chance to lose yourself in someone else's drama…or escape from your own. When you're spending hours trying to figure out how he feels…where this is going…what he meant when he said X…why he's taking so long to text back…you don't really have to face yourself. You lose yourself in the emotional high of it all. It's even better if you're dealing with a guy who comes with a lot of emotional baggage. Investing in his problems is like a vacation from dealing with your own.

But in a good relationship…a relationship where you're on the same page, where you aren't waiting anxiously for the next text, where you aren't wondering if he likes you because you know exactly how he feels…well, those are the relationships that bring you face to face with who you truly are. Sometimes they bring out the best in you, because we all have inherent goodness within us. And sometimes they bring out the worst in you, because a lot of us have been burned or are holding on to traumas from the past that we didn't even realize were still buried within us.

Sometimes there will be nothing wrong in the relationship, but you'll feel sad or anxious or upset. You won't be able to blame this on the fact that he didn't call or text, or that you're not his girlfriend or he hasn't said "I love you," because he never leaves you hanging…he is proud to call you his girl-friend…he adores you, and you know it. These feelings aren't coming from him; they're coming from you. If you've been hurt in the past, this feeling of unease comes from your own deep-seated trust issues. If regardless of his behavior you can't seem to trust that he'll be there for you, then this is your own fear of abandonment rising to he surface, and it's something you need to face yourself.

In a good relationship, your actions, your mindset, your behavior, the things you say, they all impact someone else. Sometimes you'll really hurt your partner and realize how insensitive you can be. Sometimes he'll say something inno-cent and it will cause a huge fight because that innocent comment hit an open wound of yours you didn't even know existed.

Sometimes you'll feel unloved, insecure, angry. Sometimes you'll want to just run, and sometimes you'll feel really lonely, and that will surprise you, because how can you be lonely in the company of someone who truly loves you?

Some will make the mistake of thinking this is the wrong relationship, and they'll leave. Some will blame their partner for "making" them feel a certain way, and issues will continue to arise until the relationship implodes. Others will realize that you can't let love in from the outside if you don't feel it on the inside and will do the hard inner work to get there. They will face their demons and deal with the pain from the past. They will communicate openly and honestly with their partners about their fears and their doubts, and they won't hold on to anger and resentment. They will realize that all relationships, even the best ones, take work, but it starts with working on yourself.

There's this idea that in the right relationship, everything will just be perfect. He'll be the other half of your soul, you'll reach a level of happiness you never knew existed, you'll feel secure and comfortable and confident. A good relationship can give you these things for sure, but not on its own. It has to start from within. If you don't already feel good, if you still have issues to work through, if you have a void within, you will never fully be able to trust him, and you will never truly feel "good enough." No matter how many sweet things he says or does, you will never be able to give and receive love freely.

When we're single, we're often unaware of the work that needs to be done because those parts of us that are hurt and need to be healed don't get accessed. Or maybe we do know but think the right guy will make it all better. Love forces you to face yourself. Love brings up all that is unloved within us. And you can't hide who you are when you are in a good, loving relationship. Instead, you are forced to face it and deal with it. Your partner will always reflect back who you really are (and vice versa). And everything that happens will be much more emotionally significant.

When all you've had are bad relationships, it's hard to really know what you're doing when a good one comes along. You're not used to this feeling of things just being right. You're not used to just coasting along on placid waters and you can't trust it. Instead, you stand on high alert, waiting for a storm to roll in and knock you overboard. For some of us, it might genuinely feel weird to just know how a guy feels about us and not have to guess and decode and look for clues. It can be unfamiliar, and we may take it to mean something is amiss and worry we're overlooking something. Maybe we pick him apart, maybe we start fights, maybe we feel despair because this isn't how it's supposed to be.

Someone may be perfect for you, but they still won't be a perfect person. And you're not a perfect person. And the relationship won't be perfect but it will force each of you to deal with your issues and work on yourselves to be better because in the right relationship, you want to be your best self…not just for your sake, but because you're accountable to him and you don't want to cause him any hurt and pain. But the path to becoming your best self isn't always a smooth one. There are bumps and sharp turns and it can be dark and scary sometimes…but it's OK. It's normal, in fact.

The road to becoming our best selves takes time, patience, and a lot of work. It involves gaining an awareness of what we need to work on and finding the tools to get there.

Here are a few key things you can do to make a "good" relationship even better:

1. Manage Your Thoughts

Emotionally generated thoughts tend to become magnified and then multiply. Let's say one day your wonderful, loving boyfriend doesn't text you back for hours. In the moment maybe you start to get upset and think, "I can't believe he didn't answer that sweet text I just sent him; I know he always has his phone on him and is constantly checking it. He must not care about me, or maybe he's having doubts. He never shows me he cares (then insert a running tab of all the instances, big or small, where you didn't feel cared for by him). I can't believe I'm with a guy who doesn't appreciate me, I don't deserve this," and on and on.

The more the thoughts come flooding in, the more upset you'll become. Instead of continuing down this road, cut the flow of thoughts off at the source. Shift your thinking: OK, he didn't text me back right away so it must mean he's in a meeting or got tied up. He cares about me, I know he does. He texts back right away the majority of the time. His feelings didn't suddenly change; that just wouldn't make any logical sense.

Try to identify your faulty line of thinking and gain a more objective awareness. Look for the good in him and the good in your relationship and focus on that instead of participating in a negative line of thinking that isn't serving you in any positive way.

2. Tell Him What You're Feeling

I mentioned earlier that sometimes we can suddenly feel hurt or upset by something minor. When this happens, it usually isn't the result of what's going on in the present, it's because some hurt from the past was triggered. If you find yourself feeling scared or upset, just be open and tell him.

Being vulnerable is what strengthens emotional bonds. In a healthy, loving relationship we need to trust that we can be vulnerable with our partners without them using our disclosures against us. If something happens and you feel an emotional response, tell him what's going on. Maybe you say something like, "I really care about you and I want to get closer to you, but I've been hurt badly in the past and sometimes my fear of being hurt again gets triggered."

These honest disclosures will not scare him away; if anything, they'll make him feel even closer to you and make him want to protect you from feeling these negative emotions even more. When you get angry or defensive or blame him for making you feel a certain way, then you activate his fears and his defenses and it pushes him away.

No matter what darkness you have inside, being open and honest about it and sharing it in a loving way will strengthen your bond. As long as it's done without blame or shame, you can basically tell him anything.

3. Manage Your Mood

The only person you can control is yourself. You can inspire a man to feel and do certain things, but you can never force it out of him. A lot of us fall into the role of being victims of circumstance. We let the things that happen dictate how we feel when really that's our decision to make. Yes, sometimes something will happen and you'll have an immediate emotional response, but it's up to you to decide if that incident ruins your day or not. Ultimately your mood is largely under your control.

When you bring a happy, positive mood into your interactions with your guy, it's contagious. When he experiences that positive energy, he feels happy and empowered and he wants to do more and give more and be even better in the relationship. It is only when a man feels defeated or feels like a loser who can't make his woman happy that he retreats and doesn't engage in those loving behaviors.

4. Resolve Your Issues, Don't Wait for Them to Resolve Themselves

A good relationship will always bring your unresolved issues to the surface. That's because good relationships with partners who love us force us to be at our best…and in order to be our best, we have to deal with and rid ourselves of our worst. Whether it's insecurity, poor self-esteem, fear of abandonment, or character flaws like being insensitive, impatient, or selfish…they all come out. You can try to shove them to the side, but they'll keep coming back until they are properly dealt with.

Love can be healing in some ways, but your partner is not responsible for your emotional well-being, only you are. The path to resolution will be different for everyone. Some will find the answers on their own, some may find it in a self-help book, and some will want to work with a therapist.

The worst thing you can do is nothing. Problems don't just work themselves out on their own; you won't wake up one day and discover that all your issues are gone. The greatest service you can do for yourself and your relationship is to be growth oriented and always strive to be your best self.

5. Tell Him What You Want

Even the best boyfriend or husband in the world isn't going to give you exactly what you want all the time because he doesn't always know what that is…so the best way to get it is to just tell him! Men are not responsive to nagging or criticism, but they can be enormously receptive—and appreciative—when you tell them what makes you happy in a loving way.

This feels *so* much better than being upset at him for not doing something and holding it in and silently resenting him for it. When you do that, you transmit a punishing vibe that hangs in the air and poisons everything, making him even less likely to do what you want.

We all give and experience love in different ways. Even in the best relationship, you aren't going to feel completely loved all the time. Again, some of this is the result of your own stuff and some of it is because he doesn't always know what to do to make you feel loved. When you tell him, then you free yourself from the confines of feeling resentful and unloved and he feels better because now he can rise up and be the amazing man you need and deserve. So everyone wins.

How to Stop Stressing over Your Relationships

One of the biggest relationship mistakes I see women make is stressing over their relationship, whether it's in the dating stage or in a more established relationship. The panic and trepidation they feel is almost palpable in the e-mails I receive. I tried to address the issues in an article I wrote on A New Mode, and it definitely struck a chord and sparked an avalanche of e-mails and comments from women who were feeling panicked over the state of their relationships. Most understood the point I was making in the article, but rather than relaxing and just going with the flow, they wanted to know: "How can I fix it if I was stressing too much?" "What should I text him to fix the situation?" "Is it OK if I tell him XYZ?" "Is he gone forever?" "How can I get him back?" OK, full stop. This is *exactly* the problem. The worry and the doubt and the fear and the questions. I know it feels like you're being productive by ruminating like this, but it gets you nowhere. And it definitely doesn't lead to a happy, long-lasting relationship.

When you stop stressing out over the relationship, you are free to really be in the relationship. You can see the other person for who he is, and you can give yourself to him freely – no strategies, no game-playing, no manipulation. You won't feel a need to control anything. You can just be, and there is no greater feeling than that.

But how do we do it? How do we stop our minds from spinning into overdrive, sending out waves of unpleasant thoughts and sounding alarm bells?

1. Realize Stressing Gets You Nowhere

First, you need to realize that getting all wound up over the state of your relationship serves no purpose, ever. It causes problems within the relationship but more importantly, it takes a huge toll on your sense of self and self-esteem. When you care too much, you inevitably become attached to a certain outcome. You invest mental energy in making sure things go a certain way. And if they don't, then you suffer on many levels.

I have been guilty of stressing over past relationships. It was always the same pattern. Things started out fun and light, I got excited about the possibilities…and then became scared that my imagined future wouldn't come to be…and then panic set in. From then on, the relationship was no longer enjoyable. Every interaction and conversation became a test to see exactly where he stood and how he felt.

Anyone who has dated long enough knows exactly what I'm talking about. The problem is that our minds trick us into believing there is some sort of payoff to this type of thinking. Like it will somehow lead us to a place of confidence and clarity. It won't. It will lead you in the opposite direction and cause you to feel even more uncertain and insecure.

2. See a Relationship for What It Is

Let's talk about what a relationship is and isn't. We'll start with what it isn't. A relationship isn't a measure of your worth or worthiness in this world. It is not there to serve you and give you things like happiness and self-esteem. It is not there to make you feel good about life and about yourself. This isn't to say a relationship can't do these things, it's just that these aren't the elements upon which a healthy relationship is built.

A relationship also isn't some sort of milestone, a sign that you've "made it," that you will be OK, that you are now a member of some elite club. It isn't something you work to acquire. It is not a goal to achieve.

A relationship is an experience to be had and shared. It is about discovering how compatible you are with someone else, and if there is enough chemistry and compatibility to form a lifelong partnership. The only work you have to do is to make sure you are your best self and get to a place where you can give and receive love. No amount of plotting or analyzing will change whether you and someone else are compatible. You either are or you aren't. The dating process is more of a discovery process to find out if it's there.

So you enter into the relationship as your best self and then one of two things happens: it works out, or it doesn't. And if it doesn't, you're OK because you know that it just means you weren't a match with that person. It doesn't mean you're flawed or damaged or bad or unlovable. It just wasn't a match. Sometimes you'll be able to see this, and sometimes the other person will have that clarity. Either way, if it doesn't work, it's because it wasn't the right fit. That's all!

If you can realize this, *really* realize it, then there will be absolutely nothing to stress over.

3. Set a Freak-Out Deadline

A lot of us make the mistake of prematurely freaking out over something that really turns out to be absolutely nothing. For example, let's say you start seeing a new guy and things are going great. You talk regularly, go on fun dates, it seems to be going really well. But then you don't hear from him for a day or two and immediately hit the panic button.

And then the devastation starts to creep in…followed by the doubts. What did I do wrong? Was it something I said? Something I did? Why do the guys I like always leave me? You feel a sense of dread deep in your gut and you know, you just *know*, that he's never coming back.

Meanwhile, in boy land, he's been really slammed at work and has barely had a minute to come up for air. In his mind, the relationship is going great, he's happy to have met a great girl like you and he can't wait to finish this big project so he can see you again. He's happily going along doing his thing while you are knee-deep in heartbreak mode, mourning the loss of what could have been and trying to figure out where it all went wrong.

And just when the agony is at its peak…he calls! And everything is fine! You're relieved, but at the same time, you are so *in it* now. You cling to the relationship even tighter because you remember how miserable it felt when you thought you'd lost it, and you vow not to do anything to screw this up.

I'm not saying the relationship will be doomed after this point, but I can guarantee it will cause a major shift in the dynamic and it will definitely ruin your ability to actually enjoy the relationship anymore.

Rather than reflexively panicking when something seems amiss, set a deadline. For example, if you started seeing a guy and don't hear from him for a day or two, say, "I will not panic about this right now. If I don't hear from him by X day at Y time, then I am allowed to be upset about this," and then just take it out of your mind.

This also works if you're in a more established relationship. Let's say you don't see your boyfriend as often as you'd like. Maybe you'd like to go on dates more regularly or see him a few times during the week. Tell yourself that you will be fine with things for the time being, and if nothing changes in two weeks, then you can be upset about it and deal with it. Or let's say you're in a serious relationship and there has been talk of getting engaged, but he hasn't popped the question yet. Instead of getting angry about it, just give yourself a deadline. If he doesn't propose in the next month, then I will be upset and I will deal with it. Until then, I'm going to enjoy the relationship and not let this bother me.

This little exercise will help you train your mind to stay calm and avoid spinning into a frenzy. It will help you gain control over your thoughts and your mood, and this will be of major benefit to you and your relationship. And the funny thing is, whatever problem you wanted to get really upset about right away usually resolves itself before the deadline you set! I'm telling you, it really works.

4. Be Present

The biggest problem with stressing over your relationship is that it takes you out of the relationship and into a place that's not real. When you get stressed and anxious, you're no longer interacting with the person sitting in front of you, you're interacting with the thoughts in your mind. You fixate on an imagined future and worry about how and if you'll get there with him. Stop doing this!

Instead, just be present. Be right here, right now. When you go on a date with a guy, whether it's the first or the fiftieth, all you should be thinking about is enjoying your time with him and building a connection. If you're in the early stages of dating, the only thing to decide is whether you want to go on another date with this person (and save that consideration for after the date). Don't size him up and look for signs that he's the one and this is *it*. Don't scan him to determine how he feels and if he likes you. Just enjoy it for what it is and let the process unfold organically. *No stress!*

When you worry about where this is going and if there's a future, you blind yourself to what's in front of you and hinder your chances of forming a real connection. You can't connect with someone who isn't there with you in that present moment. Most people don't see other people, they only see their concerns of the moment, and they clutter their minds trying to figure out how he feels, what he's thinking, and so forth. The concern and worry and doubt feels like it's serving a purpose, but it's not! It's actually taking you further away from where you want to be. A relationship is what's in front of you, that's it!

201

Now I'm not saying you should never think about the future or discuss where things are heading, there is a time for that. Discussing the relationship or the future isn't the problem, the problem occurs when the *mindset* you have about the relationship revolves around what you want and are afraid you won't get, instead of what you have. When you're full of anxiety and fear, and you panic thinking about what will or won't be in the future, you have an unhealthy mindset. The best way to fix this is to try to just be present. In chapter 4 we talked about how being "the prize" is less a set of behaviors than a mindset, and this is the same.

5. Stop Fixating on What Things Supposedly Mean

As women, we've all been programmed to see having a relationship as some sign that we've made it, that we're worthy. Being single is seen as something to be pitied and being in a relationship is something to covet. As a result, a lot of us measure our worth by our relationship status. If a guy leaves, that means we're unworthy and we weren't good enough to have this thing that we've been told we need in order to be good enough. It's hard to undo years of faulty programming when it's been so firmly ingrained into our psyche, but it isn't impossible.

Remember, only you can determine your own worth. You won't get a sense of your own value from a bottle or from a man or by splurging on the latest trends. *You* set the standard for how valuable you are. You do this by living a rich, fulfilling life filled with things you love. You do things that make you happy, you work on improving yourself, you develop your talents, you take care of yourself, you do things that tap into your essence and allow you to express your true self. This is how self-esteem is built. If you wrap up your identity in what men think of you, or what your relationship status is, you will never ever feel satisfied.

In any relationship, you need to have faith in yourself and trust that no matter what happens, you will be OK and you can handle whatever life throws at you. Anytime you start to panic, anytime your mind starts spinning and you worry that he'll leave, that he's losing interest, that he's not that into you and *what are you going to do if he leaves? How will you go on?* You'll be fine! You were fine before you met him and you'll be fine if he decides to leave. You are OK. Everything will be OK. Say it to yourself as many times as you need to, until it really penetrates!

Remember This

Stop freaking out! Relationships aren't that hard, they only feel hard because we stress over them for no reason and create problems when there aren't any. Everything will be OK, just relax and trust the timing of your life.

8

What Guys Want in a Woman and from a Relationship

The greatest happiness of life is the conviction that we are loved; loved for ourselves, or rather, loved in spite of ourselves.

– Victor Hugo

As I've said many times over, the most essential ingredient to having an amazing relationship is to love yourself and love your life. When you can check those things off the list, then everything else falls into place. Again, I'm not saying if it's not working out it's all your fault and all on you. A relationship is a partnership, it's about working together and creating a deep and meaningful connection. It's not about one person bending over backward to make the other happy or trying to be whatever he needs.

I've spent a lot of time talking about you, so now let's talk about *him*, specifically what he wants and needs from a relationship. Personally, I loved discovering this stuff. It made the male gender a slightly less foreign entity to me and made relationships so much more fun and enjoyable. I no longer had to bang my head against the wall trying to figure him out, I just got it. I knew what he was thinking and why he was being a certain way. I also knew what to do in order to get my needs met in the relationship. This is true of when I was single and dating around and still holds true now that I'm married. Knowledge is a powerful thing; use it wisely!

The Main Difference between Men and Women in Relationships

There are many differences between men and women, both in the way we're designed physically and the way we process things emotionally. And I'm sure you've noticed that the way we view relationships is also very different. The main problem in a lot of relationships is that women don't know what men want.

While the differences may seem vast, they're pretty simple when you break it down. Once you can understand the differences, you'll have a much easier time understanding your guy and making your relationship even more amazing.

I want to preface this by saying that I know there are exceptions. To be clear, I'm going to be speaking about the way men and women are *in general*.

In general, the appeal of a relationship for women is *the relationship*. Women naturally gravitate towards the idea of marriage and see it as highly appealing. An ideal relationship for a woman is one where she feels understood and connected to her significant other. An ideal man is one who truly *understands* her and cares for her.

The ideal relationship for a man is one where he gets to feel like the man. Men don't have the same need for understanding as women do. Rather, men like to feel acknowledged, respected, and appreciated. Men typically enjoy the role of being givers, so for a man, the ideal woman is one who can happily receive. There is nothing sexier or more appealing to him than a happy woman who appreciates everything he has to offer, not just physically, but also emotionally and intellectually.

While men love to give, they don't always know what you need and most relationship problems arise from basic communication malfunctions where a woman goes about trying to tell a man what she needs in the wrong way.

For instance, if your boyfriend or husband is hardly ever home, rather than saying: "Why aren't you ever home?" say "I really love it when you're here." If your partner isn't meeting your needs, it is always a much better strategy to tell him what you do want rather than constantly hammering in what you don't want and pointing out the ways in which he's failing to meet your needs.

Remember, he *wants* to make you happy, and the more appreciated he feels the more he will go out of his way to give you what you want.

It's also worth noting that men respond to specific compliments much better than abstract ones. For instance, saying something like: "Thank you for doing the dishes, that was so thoughtful of you" packs more of a punch than something general like "You're so thoughtful." This can be an area of confusion since women are thrilled with general compliments (you're so smart/pretty/nice/funny/etc.)

While the principles I've outlined may seem fairly straightforward and universally understood, they often get completely ignored. The biggest mistake most women make in relationships is assuming men think just like they do.

The key to a successful relationship is communicating your needs in a way that the other person can *hear*. If you attack or blame, your guy will completely shut down and tune you out. If you come from a place of compassion and appreciation, he will tune in to exactly what you're saying and will try to do whatever he can to make you happy.

It's only when we embrace our differences and see the other side more clearly that healthy communication can flourish. Try it out and you'll see what I mean!

How to Be an Amazing Girlfriend/Wife/Partner

There is so much misinformation out there about what it takes to be a great partner. It's not about cooking his favorite food or wearing sexy lingerie or mastering some crazy sexual trick. (I'm not saying these things don't help, but they don't get to the heart of the matter!) Understanding how men think and what they need in a relationship makes an enormous difference in the way you're able to relate to one another.

The top prerequisite for being in a great relationship is to be your best self. A trap that many people in relationships fall into is blaming their partner when problems arise. Rather than seeing what they can do to make things better, they blame him for not being what they want and think that if only he did XYZ, *then* everything would be fine.

It doesn't work that way. You can't ever make someone what you want them to be. All you can do is bring your best. When you do this, the other person will usually rise up and match you at your level.

While every guy has his own preferences when it comes to the physical, there are several fundamental qualities that all men crave in a woman.

Here are the most essential ways to be the most amazing partner ever:

Be Direct (Not Passive-Aggressive)

The majority of problems in a relationship occur because the woman expects a man to meet her needs and then resents him when he doesn't. She doesn't ask for what she wants because he should just "know." She may drop hints to help him out and then become even more annoyed when he doesn't pick up on them. The man, in turn, gets frustrated that nothing he does seems to be good enough. Eventually he gets discouraged and stops trying, and she feels even more resentful. Neither side has bad intentions; the problem is they aren't communicating properly because men and women have very different styles of communication. Men do not pick up on nuances and subtleties in the same way women do; they need things spelled out in a clear and direct manner.

If you're mad at him, don't act passive-aggressive until he asks what's wrong (to which you may reply "nothing," which he'll take to mean nothing is wrong, after which you'll continue to simmer because he should freakin' know it's *something*!) Just tell him what he did wrong. In relationships it's not usually what you say, it's *how* you say it. If you tell a guy something he is doing is upsetting or hurting you, and you say it in a loving, compassionate way, I guarantee he will try to fix it. If you come from a place of anger or resentment, he'll shut down and will be less motivated to correct it. Sigmund Freud is regarded as one of the most brilliant minds in psychology and even he had no idea what women want, so how do you expect the average guy to know?

Most arguments in relationships stem from deeper underlying issues that never get discussed or resolved. Maybe a woman feels like her guy doesn't really care about her, or isn't committed to her because he isn't as attentive as he was in the beginning of the relationship. Instead of being direct about it, she freaks out on him if he doesn't call her back one night or doesn't do the dishes after she slaved away cooking dinner for him. From there a big fight may ensue over something trivial while the real issue goes untouched. When you want something, or don't want something, just tell *him*.

Appreciate Him

Most women don't realize how *starved* men are for appreciation; I certainly had no idea until I started writing about relationships full time. The problem is that we usually love others the way we like to be loved, and women typically feel loved when a man is being giving and attentive to her and her needs. Because of that, many women will be extra giving to their man. While this is very nice and appreciated, it's not what men really crave.

What a man deeply desires is feeling acknowledged and appreciated for what he provides. He wants to feel like his efforts were a success. This applies to everything he does from taking you out to a fancy dinner to taking out the trash.

If he takes you out on a nice date, acknowledge and appreciate him for it and tell him you had an amazing time. Men are typically more responsive to compliments about something they've done rather than who they are, as I described in the previous section.

When a woman really sees and appreciates her man, it makes him feel like the ultimate winner and makes him want to do anything to keep her happy.

Another important relationship skill is to try to see the intention behind an action, and appreciate that. I have a personal example for this. Years ago I was dating a guy and one night he called and asked if he could come over. It was getting late and I was exhausted, but he said he'd be over in a half hour so I agreed. An hour and half later he still hadn't arrived and I was fuming! *Where could he be? Why is he even bothering to come over this late? Why do I have to wait up for him when I just need sleep!* He finally showed up carrying something that smelled delicious. I immediately went off on him for making me wait up for him and he sheepishly said, "I'm sorry, I wanted to surprise you and bring over a quesadilla from that place you love because I know you've been working so hard and barely have time to eat." Even though I was starving and had been *fiending* for a quesadilla, my anger had been building for an hour and didn't subside, and the rest of the night was uncomfortable and tense.

The mistake I made was in looking at the action (him being late), rather than the intention (him wanting to do something nice to make me happy). I'm not saying I shouldn't have been annoyed by his lateness, but the night probably would have gone a lot differently had I at least appreciated his good intentions…then later I could have nicely mentioned that the next time there was an hour-long line at the place, he should just buy me a bag of chips and call it a day!

No one is perfect and no matter how great your relationship, there will be times when he isn't doing something exactly the way you'd like him to. You'll get a lot further, and do a huge service to your relationship, if you focus on what he *is* doing right rather than focusing on what he isn't.

Give Him Space When He Needs It

Another major difference between men and woman is in the way they handle stress and difficulties. While women typically seek out their friends and want to talk about it, men would rather retreat into the proverbial man cave and deal with it on their own. A woman might get upset when this happens and think he's shutting her out, but it really has nothing to do with her—it's just how he deals with things.

If your boyfriend seems stressed out and begins to withdraw, just let him be. Don't coddle him or offer unsolicited advice or get on his case about why he isn't confiding in you. If he wants to talk about it with you, he will. If he doesn't and you continue to push him, you will just be another source of stress in his life that he needs to deal with, and he'll withdraw even further.

Men intuitively know that it isn't easy for women to give them space when they need it, so if you can do it without feeling angry or resentful, you'll be the woman who touches him more deeply than any other.

Maintain Your Own Life outside of the Relationship

This tip isn't just for his sake, it's for yours. I swear sometimes I feel like I should throw a goodbye party when a friend of mine gets a boyfriend because she'll literally fall off the map! I know I won't be seeing her at Sunday brunches or fun nights out. She won't want to come away with the girls for the weekend. Getting face time with her will never be easy, and eventually I'll give up and resign myself to the fact that I'll either see her again at her wedding or if she becomes single again (in which case, she'll be back in full force and down for anything!)

It's not just my friends; women make this mistake all the time (myself included!) They get into a relationship and the guy becomes the center of their universe. This is never healthy! For one thing, it kind of puts your relationship in a holding pattern and creates a scenario where you can be dating for years and years without taking the next step. If a guy is getting all of you, all the time, there's no reason for him to take that extra step...but that's a whole different discussion.

Another issue is that your relationship can't be your only source of happiness and fulfillment; you need to have a balanced life with several components filling you up in different areas. If you throw all of that away for your guy, then you add a lot of pressure to the relationship and will never feel completely satisfied with what you're getting from it (mostly because no one can be your everything). You may start to resent your partner and feel that he owes you more since you gave up so much for him, but that's not fair because the sacrifices you made were *your* choice. Another reason not maintaining your own life outside of the relationship is problematic is that you may end up staying in a bad relationship for far longer than you should because, well, you have nothing else to go back to.

Men typically fall in love with a woman in her absence, not her presence. If you're always there he won't experience that deepening of the bond. To keep your relationship fresh and invigorating, it's essential to have time apart to do your own things. It gives you a break from the emotional intoxication of the relationship so you can see things more objectively, and it also takes some pressure off of the relationship and allows it to unfold more organically. I know it's tempting to hang out with him every time he asks, I know it's flattering when a guy wants so much of your time, I know you may think it's because he is just so crazy about you…and maybe he is, but giving in every single time is just not a good strategy. If he's a decent guy, he'll respect your boundaries and will encourage you to do your own thing on occasion.

Take Care of Yourself

Don't stop working out, eating healthy, getting waxed, shaving your legs, blow-drying your hair, or any other healthy or beautifying activity that was a part of your life pre-relationship. Yes, it's easy to slide into a more *laissez-faire* approach when you're in a relationship, but if you do that then it won't be long before you're searching up and down to retrieve the burning spark that once existed.

Look, you don't need to be red carpet ready at all times, but you really should make an effort to try to maintain your appearance and look good for your guy. You put your best face forward during those first few months of dating, and there's no reason for it to stop once things are more established. It will keep the passion and lust alive in your relationship and also, it makes a man feel really good when a woman puts in effort to look beautiful for him.

The funny thing I notice is that women in relationships (again, myself included), will lounge around the house in sweats and a messy bun and no makeup when they're home with their guy, but will put on a face-full of makeup and get decked out when going out…to impress strangers? The whole thing is so backwards. A guy friend once lamented to me that his girlfriend had put on about 15 pounds since they'd started dating and canceled her gym membership. He told me he was still very much attracted to her, but he just couldn't under-stand why she wasn't taking care of herself anymore, and that was more of a turn-off than the weight gain. He felt stuck because there was no way to say something without her being offended and hurt. He pleaded with me to spread the gospel and tell women that while a man's love isn't solely contingent on physical appearance, it's really important (and attractive) to continue to take care of yourself like you did when you first met…and so I have!

Smile!

This is another tip that will enormously help your relationship, but also your life in general. Men cannot resist a woman with a smile. In fact, every guy I know has said that a positive attitude is the number-one most attractive quality a woman can have. Look, life isn't always going to be rainbows and sunshine. Sometimes the poop hits the fan, but your life will be a much better place overall if you can tackle it all with a smile and the conviction that it will all work out.

This kind of energy is infectious. It draws people towards you and it makes you the kind of woman a man will want to be with forever. Don't use your guy as a sounding board or your relationship as an emotional dumping ground. When your guy comes home, greet him with a smile...and then vent if you had a rough day and need to let it out.

Try to see the good in all situations, both in your relationship and outside of it. The things that happen in our lives, for the most part, are neutral. What makes them good or bad is our perceptions and the thoughts we attach to them.

Respect Your Man

It goes without saying that an ideal woman is one who respects herself, but she also genuinely respects her man.

In addition to needing to be appreciated, men have an enormous need to feel respected. This is true of all humans, but usually this desire burns stronger in men. A man feel respected when a woman appreciates who he is and what he needs and gives him space to express himself without making demands on him and prioritizing herself over him.

Respect means accepting that he needs certain things, even if they are in opposition to what *you* want or need. For example, when men get stressed or feel unbalanced, they usually like to retreat into their "cave" to sort things out. They don't necessarily like talking through the problem and would rather work it out on their own and then come back into the relationship re-charged.

So let's say your guy is having a hard time and needs some time alone, but you really want him to be open and honest with you and to share his feelings. Respecting him entails putting what's best for him above what you want. In this case, it would be giving him the space to work through his issues even though you would prefer that he talk to you about it, because that's what's going to be most beneficial for him.

It also means respecting who he is, how he lives his life, and what his opinions are. Respect does not look like rolling your eyes when he says something you don't agree with (or think is the dumbest thing you've ever heard) and it doesn't look like not at least hearing him out and validating his opinion. It's never nice or fair to make someone feel like an idiot just because you don't quite see where they're coming from, and a really important skill is being able to listen to and respect another person's.

Respect Yourself

A man cannot love or care for a woman unless he respects her—it just won't happen. And a man cannot genuinely respect a woman who will put up with anything. While in theory a man would love to get away with everything, in reality there is nothing interesting or appealing about it. A lot of women are afraid to be firm in their convictions because they don't want to seem demanding or needy (which is funny because only needy people compromise on what they want).

Bending over backwards for a guy and letting him get away with treating you badly because you don't want to seem like a nag will guarantee more bad behavior, and eventually it will take a big hit on your sense of self. So figure out what you want and what you won't compromise on. And don't be afraid to walk away when he doesn't give you what you know you deserve. It's only when you're not afraid to walk away that he'll do anything to make you stay.

Putting up with poor treatment indicates you don't respect yourself. Each time you accept and forgive him for bad behavior, you are actually enforcing that it's OK for him to treat you badly.

At the core of having self-respect is having healthy boundaries. Having strong boundaries means you prioritize your needs and your emotions and do not assume responsibility for someone else's needs and emotions. When a woman has strong boundaries, she demonstrates confidence, self-respect, and a high sense of self-worth. Weak boundaries, on the other hand, are a sign of insecurity and low self-esteem.

If you don't have strong boundaries, a man doesn't have to work to get you. He can have you whenever he wants; you'll drop what you're doing to see him, you'll work around his schedule, his needs will suddenly become your needs. A guy might stick around for this, but this is not the kind of woman a man yearns for and deeply commits to.

A woman with healthy boundaries will not lose herself in a relationship and will not allow her identity to be entirely contingent upon how he sees her. She brings her best self to the relationship, and if problems arise she doesn't blame herself and assume the responsibility for solving them. She acts in accordance with who she is and what she believes, and doesn't modify who she is for the sake of getting a guy or keeping him interested.

What Bad Boundaries Look Like

Heather was dating Ray for about a year, and their relationship was great aside from the fact that he wouldn't call her his girlfriend. The entire relationship was also operating according to his schedule. He had a stressful job and would work extremely long hours so she reasoned that it was only natural that they plan their time together around his schedule. If he had a night off, she would cancel whatever plans she had in order to see him. Sometimes he would disappear for days at a time with no explanation. If she called him out on it, he would get angry at her and remind her that they were not an official item and he could do as he pleased.

If she wanted to see him and he was busy, he would get annoyed. But if he wanted to see her, then he *had* to see her, and would call and text nonstop until she answered.

One night she was on a date with a new guy who had potential, but he was extremely turned off by the fact that her phone was blowing up the entire time. When she would confront Ray about how unreasonable it was for him to be able to do whatever he wanted, sometimes disappearing for days at a time, then get angry and upset when she wasn't available, he would turn everything around on her until she ended up apologizing to *him*. She finally got the strength to tell him that she could no longer continue seeing him if he didn't make a commitment, and even though he was upset, he let her go. Within a few weeks he was calling her again and asking to see her…and she would agree. (I can't help it! she'd exclaim. I love him and want to see him.) She was there for him whenever he needed her. Even at 4 AM, if he wanted to see her, she would be there. But he was not always there when she needed him. Sometimes he would disappear and ignore her calls for weeks or even months. Then he would re-emerge and demand all her attention. And she always gave in.

After two years when Ray was in one of his disappearance modes she finally started to move on and began seeing someone new. Like clockwork, he re-emerged. After she ignored his calls for weeks, he showed up at her door, demanding to know why she'd been ignoring him. She told him she was seeing someone new, and he broke down and tearfully said he loved her. She felt bad for him and gave him another chance (by now, this would have been his 500th). He still wouldn't commit, still did whatever he wanted, still didn't respect her needs or her time, still was the exact same person. She has since attempted to cut it off many more times, but it never sticks. Why? Because she has no boundaries and puts his needs and his hurts above her own. Don't be like this!

Encourage Him to Meet Your Needs...without Being Needy

While some of your previous relationships may have proven otherwise, the truth is men are natural givers. Yes, that's right. They want to give, they want to provide, and they want to make you happy. What they don't want is to be bossed around and told what to do.

When a woman tells a man what to do, she is essentially emasculating him by taking away the very thing that makes him feel significant: his ability to provide. When you boss him around, he feels like a failure for not being able to do his job. Rather than wanting to do more for you, he feels defeated and retreats.

I'm not saying you should just let him do whatever he wants and not say a peep. There is a right way to encourage a guy to meet your fundamental needs (when I say needs, I mean universal needs we have as humans, like the desire to bond, connect, and support each other, not texting every hour on the hour), but it has to be done in a way that empowers him, not in a way that makes him feel like a failure.

If you appreciate your man and are able to see him for who he is and love him for being that person, flaws and all, you are empowering him. When a woman is in a good place emotionally, she can empower her man effortlessly because it comes naturally to her. She brings out the best in him because she is coming from a place of love, not a place of control. She doesn't need him to validate her sense of self or be the one to heal her from her painful past. She is with him because she *wants* to be, not because she has some agenda.

Men want to feel manly and significant. They want to provide for you; it's just in their nature to be that way. However, a man will only want to give to a woman who can happily receive what he has to offer, not one who is going to make unnecessary demands in order to feel good about herself and secure in the relationship. A woman who tries to get this assurance from the outside will always be unsatisfied, and there is nothing more unappealing to a man than an unhappy woman.

Accept Him for Who He Is and Bring out His Best.

Often women get caught up in trying to turn a guy into what they want rather than accepting him as he is and encouraging him to become his best self.

Men can sense when women are trying to change or control them, and it isn't motivating—it's crippling and defeating. It makes men feel like failures and spurs them do the opposite of what you wanted. In any relationship, it's imperative to accept other people for who they are, the good and the bad. The worst thing you can do is to try to turn him into what you need him to be. It may sound crazy, but women do this all the time!

Maybe you're trying to get him to be more emotionally supportive, more sensitive, more affectionate. I mean, all these things are great, but what you need to ask yourself is, are you trying to get him to be that way because it would be good for him or because it would be good for you? Now there's the million-dollar question…

An ideal woman accepts a man as he is, and since she is

so accepting and appreciative he becomes a better man and a better partner, completely on his own. She brings her best self to the table and knows that by doing this, she will bring out his best self.

Be Confident and Secure in Yourself

This is perhaps the most essential imperative of all. In fact, if you can master this, doing everything else on this list will be easy and effortless.

There is nothing sexier or more appealing to a man than a woman who is thoroughly confident and truly loves her life. Period.

Train yourself to see the good in who you are and what you have to offer. Learn to realize that any man would be beyond lucky to land you. See yourself as the ultimate prize. Even if you don't actually feel this way yet, say it to yourself anyway. Thoughts have a way of becoming reality, and eventually it will sink it.

5 Things Guys Secretly Want from You but Will Never Ask for

One key difference I've observed between men and women is that women seem to be much more aware of what they want and need in a relationship...and aren't afraid to express it. Men, for various reasons, aren't always so in tune with what they really need in order to feel loved and fulfilled in a relationship, and the ones who are aware will seldom come right out and say it.

It makes sense from an intellectual standpoint. From an early age women learn to cultivate close, intimate relationships, and from that they learn what makes them feel cared for and understood. Male friendships don't usually have the same depth and level of closeness, so men typically enter the realm of emotional awareness later in life, usually when they form relationships with women.

A guy generally won't ask for what he needs because much of the time he doesn't even know what it is. But when you give it to him, it feels amazing. He feels appreciated and loved, and he comes to love you even more.

And with that, here are the top five things guys secretly love and want from you but will seldom ask for.

1. Compliments

No man will ever come right out and tell you that he likes it when you compliment him, because it's a weird thing to ask for and also not very "manly," if you will. But just because he doesn't ask doesn't mean he doesn't crave.

Men also feel insecure about their physical appearance, but they don't get nearly as much validation as we do. Think about it, when a guy posts a picture on Facebook or goes out with friends, he doesn't have a loyal band of cheerleaders commenting on how great he looks. When it comes to his physical appearance, you're really his only source of compliments, so load him up! Tell him you think that shirt is sexy on him, that you can tell he's been working out hard at the gym, that a certain color makes his eyes look even more striking, that his hair looks sexy pushed back…you get the point!

2. When You Ask for His Advice

You know how amazing it feels when your man cherishes and adores you and showers you with love? Well he gets the same feeling when you ask for his advice. Men have an overwhelming need to feel useful, to feel like they have something of value to offer. This is true in all areas of his life and especially so in his relationships. He wants to feel like he is adding to your life in a meaningful way, and you can help him feel this way by soliciting his advice and opinions.

When I get relationship questions from readers I love sharing them with my husband just to get his take and insights. Usually I already know the answer to the problem (I've been doing this for quite a while now!) but I still love sharing it with him and getting his feedback. And he absolutely lights up when given the chance to offer his input.

Men in general are very solution oriented and thrive when there is something to be solved. That's why a man will typically try to solve your problems when you talk to him about something that's upsetting you. Most women get frustrated by this because all we really want in those moments is emotional support, while men don't realize that giving said support is more of a solution to the problem than actually solving the problem! (If your guy does this, try not to get angry at him, just kindly tell him you appreciate his advice, but right now you just want his emotional support.)

3. When you Desire Him

You don't always need to wait for him to initiate physical affection. Men love feeling like they're irresistible—like you are turned on by them and can't get enough—so flirt with him, seduce him, initiate physical intimacy. A huge turn-on for a man is seeing how turned on his woman is by him!

4. When You Tell Him What You Want in a Way That Makes Him Feel Good

Men want to make the woman they're with happy; this is actually one of the biggest driving forces for a man in a relationship. In fact, if a man doesn't think he can make a particular woman happy, he most likely won't want to continue a relationship with her. And men appreciate it when you tell them how to make you happy, as long as it's done in the right way. The right way does not include nagging, guilting, lecturing, or shaming. It entails lovingly telling him what you like and what you want in a way that makes him feel good. Framing something as, "I really love it when you…" rather than "Why don't you ever…" is a good place to start.

When you lecture a man or come down on him for what he's doing wrong, he feels like a failure. He also feels like a little kid being scolded by mommy for misbehaving. When you tell him what you want in positive way, framing it in terms of what he's doing right, he feels good about doing it and good about himself because he knows how to make you happy.

5. Support

One of the greatest feelings to a man in a relationship is feeling like he has a woman in his corner, someone who believes in him no matter what and sees him for the great man he is and the amazing man he could be. There is comfort in knowing that you will be there for him even if he fails, especially since failure is the hardest thing for men to deal with. When you support him and believe in him, and it comes from a true and genuine place, he feels on top of the world, like he can do anything. Most women don't realize the enormous impact our approval has on men; in fact, I would say your guy is starving for your approval. When you're proud of him, it's a huge driving force that makes him feel like a winner. Conversely, when you're disappointed in him, it's crippling and makes him feel like a worthless loser.

It All Really Comes Down to…

All the five things listed actually fall under the umbrella of the number-one thing all men want but will never tell you about, the concept that has come up over and over again in this book and that is… appreciation.

Appreciation is probably the biggest motivator for a man. In order to keep your relationship happy and fulfilling, it's crucial to express appreciation for all the things he does, both big and small. As I mentioned, men are starved for your approval and they need to feel like winners. When you express genuine appreciation, you're killing two birds with one stone and giving him the greatest gift you can give. The worst thing you can do is to expect certain things from him or act entitled.

Appreciation isn't just about what he does for you, it's about appreciating who he is. Show appreciation for his good qualities, his values, his ambitions, his life choices. Find those things you love about him and show him you appreciate them. Don't assume he just knows, because he doesn't. This is probably the most powerful and transformative relationship skill that you can ever master.

The Number-One Thing Every Woman Needs to Know about Men

I constantly get asked to share the number one thing I've learned about men since I got into this business. I also wrote a book called *10 Things Every Woman Needs to Know About Men*, and when it came out the only question I got asked was: "So what's the number-one thing I need to know?"

I used to have a few answers to this question, but in recent years it's become clear to me that there really is only one. There is one core thing to understand about men, and when you get it, everything else makes sense. It is the one thing that changed my relationship when I really realized what it means.

What it comes down to is how vital it is for a man to feel like a winner in the world. You may have heard this before, especially if you're an ANM reader (and if you read my last book which really hammered this in!) but there is such a difference between hearing something and internalizing it.

A man's need to feel like a winner colors everything he

does. It's the reason he doesn't text back, it's the reason he withdraws, it's the reason he won't commit, it's the reason he doesn't give you the love you want.

How, you ask?

Men are typically goal oriented and focused. This is something we've all heard before, and most women know that men aren't as skilled at multitasking as we are. But let's go deeper and look at the reason.

The reason men are so focused and single-minded is because a man gains his sense of significance based on his ability to have an impact on the world. This doesn't mean relationships aren't important to men (they are), but in order for a man to feel good about himself and his life, he needs to feel like a winner. And when he feels like a winner, he can be the best man possible in a relationship. When he feels like a winner, he is at his absolute best. When he feels like a loser, he is at his absolute worst.

Even though I knew all about this concept, that didn't stop me from making my now husband feel like a loser when we were engaged and going through a rough patch. I couldn't quite help it. It was a stressful time and I felt like he was adding to my stress instead of helping me to alleviate it.

I know that I can be a direct, harsh, sometimes critical person. I see it as being a perfectionist, as striving for excellence. Sometimes this is a good thing, but other times it can be a very negative thing.

When I was engaged and dealing with all the stress that comes with planning a wedding, I moved on my own into our new apartment a few months before the big day and was greeted by something out of a horror movie: it was massively infested with roaches.

It was awful and disgusting and I was barely sleeping or eating, and I became angry and resentful because I didn't think he was being sympathetic or supportive enough based on what I had to deal with (his comment, "Relax, they're just bugs," really pushed me to a new level of seeing red).

I also felt like he was making wedding planning more stressful. He gave me a hard time about almost every aspect of the wedding, and I got mad at him for being so difficult and unsupportive. I was also mad that he wasn't as loving towards me as he used to be and that he now seemed uncomfortable around me. I was having a hard time and just needed him to be nice to me!

OK, long story short, we were both at fault in our own way. Both of us were being difficult and neither one of us was being empathetic to the other.

Things changed one day when, for once, we were discussing our issues lovingly and without blame and resentment, and he said to me, "I feel like I'm always failing you. Like I can never do anything right and everything I do is going to upset you or make you disappointed in me. That's why it's hard for me to be loving and comfortable around you."

It was a big slap-in-the-face moment. Here I was, this wise and worldly relationships expert, writing about how important it is to show a man appreciation and how important it is for a man to feel like a winner, and I was making the love of my life feel like a worthless loser.

I'm not saying he was totally innocent; he did do things that hurt me and he made a difficult time in my life even more difficult, but I still didn't handle it right.

I would get mad at him for expressing his feelings because it stressed me out, when really I should have listened to and acknowledged him. I didn't see the good intentions behind the ways he was trying to be there for me because I was so mad about all the things he was doing that I didn't like.

After we had that talk, I shifted gears and instead of making him feel bad about what he wasn't doing right, I lovingly showed my appreciation for what he was doing right. (This ties into a concept I've mentioned several times throughout this book: the only person you can change is yourself. I could have stayed mad and simmered in resentment because of what he did wrong, but where would that have gotten us?)

When a man feels like he's "winning" at making you happy, he goes out of his way to make you happy. After I changed my response to him, the entire relationship dynamic changed. He was so sweet and loving and so supportive and helpful in dealing with our unwanted houseguests. While at first the roaches put a strain on our relationship, once we started communicating properly and giving each other what the other needed (for him, feeling like a winner; for me, getting support and empathy), the whole ordeal ended up bringing us closer...seriously!

This is just one little example that illustrates a much larger point.

Resentment is poison for a relationship. Maybe you're mad at him and maybe it's justified, but harshly criticizing him or focusing on the negative will only make him feel like a loser. Once he feels like a loser, he'll start resenting you, which will in turn cause him to do things that make you resent him, and the cycle will continue. Someone needs to be the one to put a stop to it. While it isn't always easy, it is so worth it and will make such an incredible difference in your relationship. Being compassionate and loving is always the solution. Being negative and critical always causes more problems than it solves.

How Gratitude Changes Everything

One of the first life lessons little kids are taught is to always say, "Thank you." When people do something nice for you, you thank them. It's a concept that is drummed into our heads starting at the age of about two. But you'll notice that saying thanks doesn't always come easily. Very rarely does a kid remember to say it—it usually follows a prompt by a parent...*now what do you say?* And it never gets easier.

Gratitude doesn't come easily or naturally to most of us; rather, it's a skill that needs to be honed and crafted. But when you get it down, it can literally change your life. Countless studies have demonstrated that expressing gratitude can vastly increase our physical and emotional well-being.

Gratitude can also have enormous implications for your relationship...and your ability to find love if you aren't currently in a relationship. When both partners see the good in one another and feel appreciative, the relationship is filled with love, connection, and harmony. When one or both partners focus on what the other isn't doing and take each other for granted, the relationship is filled with resentment, frustration, and bitterness.

A good relationship starts with you. When you bring positivity and happiness into the relationship, your partner will rise up to match it, and then your relationship will flourish.

If you want your life and your relationship to improve, you can't blame circumstances or your partner. Instead, you need to take responsibility and make internal changes that lead to external ones. And the most important lesson is that of giving thanks.

Why Is It So Hard to Appreciate?

Life can tear a lot of us down. As the years go by, bitter experiences pile up and our hearts become shrouded with hurt and pain. The more jaded we become, the harder it is to see beyond the darkness and feel thankful for anything. A lot of us turn ourselves into victims in the story of our own lives, and we feel justified in doing this: we blame our parents, our upbringing, the boy who broke our heart, the bad economy. I'm not saying none of it is valid, but when you dwell on all the bad hands you've been dealt, you fuel the fire of anger and resentment, and this only makes for an even more miserable experience.

When it comes to relationships, expressing gratitude can be even more challenging because the stakes are so much higher. Romantic relationships can cause many emotions to rise to the surface...some are good and exhilarating, and some are bad and rooted in pain from the past. All of us look at life through a lens that is colored by our own experiences and we form certain expectations as a result. When you measure a guy against this code of expected behavior, he will always fall short and you will always feel disappointed. The reason he'll fall short is because no one can get it right every single time. He isn't a mind reader, and he has been shaped by a whole different set of experiences.

When you think a guy should do something and if he doesn't it means he doesn't care, then you ignore all the things he is doing to show he cares. You get all riled up because of a few things that you (or rather, your unconscious mind) think a man should do when he loves a woman. You feel hurt and unloved and might start blaming him for "making" you feel a certain way. When you're in this headspace, you will not be able to appreciate anything he does and will silently resent him for not doing more. He can text you back promptly every single time and you will still get upset the one time he takes a little longer to get back to you.

When You Appreciate a Man...

Everyone likes appreciation; we all want to be seen and acknowledged for what we do. But appreciation hits different notes for men and women. Typically, women want to feel adored and cherished above anything else in order to feel happy in a relationship. Men need to feel appreciated and acknowledged. If a man doesn't feel that, he will either leave the relationship or stay in it and feel miserable.

When a man feels like a woman appreciates him, he will go above and beyond to make her happy. It's not just about appreciating what he does, it's about appreciating *who he is*. What a man wants more than anything is a woman who is happy with him. That's really it. And a woman who expresses gratitude and is happy with who he is and what he does is the woman he wants to commit himself to.

The more gratitude you feel for him, the more connected he will feel to you and the more he will come to appreciate you. I'm not saying you're never allowed to be disappointed or upset with him, but there is a difference between disapproving of an action and disapproving of a person. You can express your discontent in a loving way that still conveys an appreciation for his character, as opposed to conveying it in a punishing and blaming way that makes him feel bad or guilty. For example, "I know you didn't mean it, I know you were only trying to be helpful, but sometimes I just need you to hear me out and give me a hug when I'm venting about something upsetting that happened."

The fact is, he really isn't *trying* to hurt you, but sometimes things he does will make you upset. And sometimes things you do will make him upset. When addressing a problem, it's best to keep in mind that neither person is intentionally trying to upset the other.

If you want more love from your man, you need to make him feel loved. The way to do this is to show genuine appreciation for the things he does. Look at the intention, not the action. He's not going to get it right every single time—that just isn't possible. But the majority of the time, his intentions are good. He set out to make you happy, and that deserves to be appreciated. You don't need to give him anything in return; just you being happy with who he is and what he does is all he needs from you.

Here are some examples of emotional hot phrases for a man (obviously they will vary depending on the man):

- I really admire how dedicated you are to your job and appreciate how hard you work.

- You are so committed to causes that are meaningful to you, and it's really admirable.

- I love that you can walk into a room and be best friends with total strangers, it's such a unique gift.

I appreciate how hard you try to make me happy. I know I don't always show it, but I notice it and it means so much to me.

- Thank you for being so helpful around the house, you really go above and beyond and I don't know what I would do without you.

And if you get stuck…this one is always a winner:

- I admire the man that you are.

How to Train Yourself to Be More Grateful

Now that we've covered why it's important to be grateful, let's talk about tangible ways to do it.

I think the most powerful way to retrain your mind to be more grateful is to keep a gratitude journal. A teacher of mine gave me this suggestion many years ago, and I thought it was the most ridiculous thing I'd ever heard. I considered myself a very grateful person and did not see how it would benefit me at all. But I gave it a try nevertheless, and wow…it was not as easy as I expected. My teacher told me to write down three things I was grateful for every day. Easy enough. The catch was that they always had to be different, as in no reruns.

As the days passed and the exercise got a little more difficult, I noticed myself changing. I started to live every day actively looking for things to be grateful for. Usually this was because I wanted to come up with three things and just be done with it, like getting in an early morning workout. I thought it would only continue to get harder, but a funny thing happened after a few weeks…it actually got easier. And soon, I was finding way more than just three new things to be grateful for each day. I kept going with this for months and can affirm that it is absolutely life-changing. I felt so calm and so at ease and just happier all around.

If you're having trouble in your relationship, I highly suggest you think of two or three things every day that you love and appreciate about your partner. You don't even need to tell him you're doing it or what the things are. Just think about it every day and write it down. And like I did in my exercise, think of new things every day. It can be things he did for you or things about him. Focus on everything he does right, and see how it impacts your relationship. (Mark my word, you'll start seeing major changes within about a week or two.)

Even if you aren't having major issues in your relationship, anytime your partner does something that annoys or frustrates you, just think about a few reasons why you care about him and why you're grateful to have him in your life.

I just want to add that this does not apply to relationships where there is physical or emotional abuse. I'm talking about healthy, functioning relationships that just get rocky from time to time...as most relationships do.

If you're single, think about what you love about your life right now. Think about what you appreciate and the good things that happen throughout the day. I think writing it out is best because it makes it more real, but if that feels like too much of a commitment then just spend time every day reflecting on it.

Practicing gratitude on a daily basis can literally rewire you. It can transform the way you think, which will change the way you feel and the vibe you transmit. People can naturally pick up on the vibes someone is sending out. When you feel bitter or angry or jaded on the inside, it will come across on the outside no matter how you try to hide it. There is no faking being in a good place. You have to work on it, and if you do, suddenly everything will change and you'll notice enormous improvements in all areas of your life.

Remember This

Men aren't monsters looking to break your heart. They also have needs and vulnerabilities. The real way to a man's heart is to appreciate him and empower him. The easiest way to do this is to train yourself to see the good, both in him and in your life in general.

9

What Pushes Men Away

Freedom is not the absence of commitments, but the ability to choose—and commit myself to—what is best for me.

– Paulo Coelho

Almost every woman has experienced the panic and uncertainty that occur when her man starts pulling away or withdrawing. Maybe it happens out of the blue or maybe something sparks it, but either way it's a miserable feeling, one that leaves you feeling powerless and painfully insecure.

It can happen in the early stages of dating, in an established relationship, or even in a marriage. Suddenly, your sweet, attentive man is a shadow that you can't quite grasp. You try to reach him, but it doesn't work. Is it something you did? Does he not care about you anymore? What is going on?!

In this section, we are going to look deeper into why men withdraw and what you can do about it.

Man-Repelling Behaviors

Before we talk about why guys pull away or withdraw, let's talk about some common behaviors that push men away. The one thing I've noticed over the years as a relationship writer is that most women have no idea how they come across to men. They may do things in an attempt to win affection and be completely baffled when their efforts produce the opposite result.

My main source of information for the articles I write is men themselves. Over the years, I've noticed a few recurring themes when it comes to things women do that completely turn guys off.

Here are the top 10 ways to repel a guy:

1. You Brag

Confidence is a major turn-on. Arrogance is not. People are inherently repelled by braggers. I'm sure your efforts are coming from a desire to impress him, but too much showing off will actually repel him. Also, asserting your all-mightiness will make him feel like you're the type of person who will always need to get her way and will never admit to being wrong, and no guy wants to deal with that.

2. You're Negative

Having a negative outlook isn't just a man-repeller, it's a people-repeller. We all have our own crap to deal with on a daily basis, and the last thing anyone needs is to get weighed down by someone else's issues and negativity.

3. You Don't "Get" Him

Most men just want to be seen and appreciated. When a man feels this from a woman, he'll want to be around her more. Conversely, when he senses she needs him, or is just trying to get something out of him in order to fulfill her own desire, he will instinctively pull away.

4. You're Critical or Put Him Down

No one likes to be criticized, but men are particularly sensitive in this area; the male ego is not something to be messed with. A man's greatest need is to feel significant and to feel like a winner in the world. If you make him feel like a loser, he won't want to be anywhere near you.

5. You Fixate on Labels or a Relationship Status

Men like to be in the moment and they don't want to feel like they're in a relationship pressure cooker where they have to meet deadlines and hit certain marks at the right time or the girl will get upset. Your focus should be on connecting with the other person and determining if this relationship is the right fit, not on getting the title for the sake of having it.

6. You're Manipulative

A guy can sense when he's being manipulated and he'll resent it. Don't do things to intentionally provoke him and get a certain reaction or response from him, this is just immature.

Healthy relationships are built on open, honest communication.

7. You're Unhappy

The sexiest woman to a guy is a happy woman. If you hate your life, your friends, yourself, he'll be repelled. Guys like to keep their lives easy and drama free.

8. You're Unpleasant to Be around

If a guy feels like hanging out with you is something he's going to have to "deal with" as opposed to something he enjoys, he won't want to do it anymore. A lot of women make the mistake of turning their relationship into a dumping ground where they can unload all their issues. While it's fine to vent to your guy on occasion, if you're constantly going to him to complain about everything in your life then being with you will become a burden.

9. You're Cruel or Mean to Others

In movies, girls like Regina George are capable of snagging the hottest guy around. In real life, there is nothing sexy about a mean girl; in fact, it's incredibly off putting. Mean people are generally unhappy people (as they say, misery loves company). Being mean also reeks of insecurity and emotional issues, two things that no man wants to deal with.

10. You're Combative

It's fine to have opinions and assert yourself as long as you can also see things from the other person's perspective and don't need to be right just for the sake of being right. A lot of women go into relationships seeing their guy as an adversary instead of a partner. The need to fight with him can have a variety of root causes, and your best bet is to identify it and find out what you're really fighting about.

When a Man Needs Space

Few things are as frightening or nerve-wracking as a man needing space. Maybe he comes right out and tells you he needs some space, or maybe you notice he's backing away...you haven't seen him in a while, his texts or calls are shorter and less frequent, and you just feel in your gut that something is amiss.

If you ask him what's going on and why he's being this way, he might come right out and say he needs some space (which does nothing to assuage your mounting anxiety), or he might say something to indicate it in an indirect way, like he needs to focus on work right now, or he's really stressed, or he thinks you should be spending some time focusing on yourself. Even worse, he may pretend like everything is totally normal, making you feel crazy, even though you know you're not crazy and something is just not right here!

A man might ask for space in the beginning of a relationship, or when things are more serious, or even after you're married. No matter what, it's a horrible feeling and you can't stop your mind from spinning and fearing the worst. You try to figure out what you could have done wrong, and you strategize about ways to make things better and get the relationship back on track. This usually doesn't work; if anything it makes the situation even worse.

Here's the thing that's important to realize: men are not women. The way they process and experience things is different. Taking space is a natural coping mechanism for most men, just as seeking out support from friends and loved ones is a natural coping mechanism for most women.

When a man needs space, it often has little, if anything, to do with you.

But let's get into it a little deeper and look at common reasons and scenarios where men need space, and what you can do about it.

He's Stressed

The number-one reason a man pulls away is because he is stressed. The source of his stress could be the result of some issue in the relationship, but it might not have anything to do with you at all.

Men don't typically like to talk about their problems—they see it as a sign of weakness. A man prides himself on being able to solve issues and can feel extremely unsettled and off balance when problems emerge in his own life that he's not able to resolve. Men will typically view themselves as weak and incapable if they voice their feelings or lean on other people for help or support. A guy might do it, but he'll typically feel like a loser or weakling for asking for support or even talking about his feelings. The way women handle difficult emotions is probably much more psychologically healthy and healing, but it is what it is.

To cope with whatever stress he is facing, a man will typically withdraw and go deep into what has become known as a metaphorical "man cave." He will want to hide himself away until he has reached a solution. This doesn't necessarily mean he's sitting down and strategizing about ways to solve the problem. Sometimes he'll just immerse himself completely in something else, like playing video games for hours on end, working, or watching sports.

Men have a much harder time processing and handling emotions than women do. They don't have the same kinds of support systems, and sharing their innermost thoughts and feelings just doesn't come naturally to them. For him, escaping from his feelings temporarily is sometimes more beneficial than trying to sort through them.

What to do: One of the biggest mistakes a woman can make when he's in this mode is to force him to talk about it. Even worse is when she tries to solve the problem for him.

Even though your intentions are pure, when you offer up solutions he feels emasculated. Men need to feel like they are in charge of their lives, like they are capable of solving whatever comes up. He prides himself on being able to solve things, and when you try to do it for him he gets the message that you don't trust that he'll be able to figure it out on his own, and it makes him feel even worse.

When he's under stress, just give him space and try not to take it personally. If you get angry or frustrated with him, he'll just see you as another source of stress in his life, and it will put more strain on the relationship.

Why is this so hard? Even though most women know about the "man cave," they still have a hard time accepting it because women cope with stress very differently. When a woman is upset, she will typically want to talk about it with those she feels closest to. Talking about it is therapeutic, and a solution isn't necessary.

Because of this, if a man doesn't want to talk about his problems, the woman can take it to mean that he doesn't feel close to her, or doesn't fully trust her or care about her. She feels shut out and rejected and may come to resent him for it, thus exacerbating any problems that already exists. It's important to realize that when a man pulls back because he's stressed, he isn't shutting you out. It's just his process, and he will be back and better than ever once he has a handle on whatever it going on.

If he does come to you, don't try to solve the problem for him. Just listen. You can offer advice if he asks, but *only* if he asks.

Space in a Committed Relationship

Another main reason a guy can need to take space in a relationship is if his needs aren't being met or he feels unappreciated. Guys aren't always able to articulate their emotional needs. It could be because they've been conditioned by society not to talk about such things or because they don't have the language to express what they want and need. Some men don't even realize their own emotional deficits, and that is an area where you can be a huge help to him!

A man won't always come right out and tell you what he needs from you, but he will know it when he gets it. So he might not tell you that he really needs your approval and appreciation. Maybe you do show him appreciation, but he needs more and he doesn't know how to tell you that. Instead, he backs away. He isn't as present or engaged, and you feel a palpable space forming and don't know how to break through.

What to do: Try to pay attention to what lights him up and what shuts him down. If he is already deep in the "man cave," engage in an open, empathetic dialogue and ask him what you could do more of to make him feel good. You might be surprised by what he tells you. And no matter what it is, try not to get defensive. Your instinctive response might be, "I do that all the time!" but try to restrain yourself and hear him out.

You can also voice what you need from him. In any relationship it's important to check in with your partner to make sure both people are happy and getting what they need to feel loved. When you approach him from a place of genuinely wanting to make the relationship better and wanting to make him feel loved, he will be receptive to you.

Space in the Beginning of a Relationship

Many women, myself included, have been in situations where they're dating a guy, things are going great, they're spending more and more time together, getting closer and closer...and then he starts pulling away. He might say he needs space, or he might just start taking it without warning. And the woman is baffled. What went wrong? She thought everything was going so well!

These situations usually happen for one of two reasons. The first is a very subtle, sneaky one. It comes from a mindset shift that happens within you. When a relationship starts to get a lot more serious, a lot of women reflexively freak out and become consumed with the fear that things won't work out. This fear causes them to cling tighter to the relationship and to associate their self-worth with how the guy feels. They think about the relationship constantly, obsess over what things mean, and analyze the "signs" looking for bad omens.

The guy can pick up on this energy. Maybe you're being subtle, but he'll feel it on a visceral level. All of a sudden he doesn't feel as relaxed around you, and the vibe is no longer fun and carefree. Instead he feels like he's being analyzed, like something is expected of him, like you don't fully trust him…and it's a bad feeling. He might not be able to pinpoint it, but suddenly he doesn't feel as strong of a pull to be around you.

What to do: Don't stress, everything is fine! Your fears are real; I'm not taking away from that. It could be because you've dated guys in the past who ended it out of the blue, and you're afraid of being in the same situation again. You might not have a solid sense of self-esteem and so you look to men to fill up your self-worthy tank. Try to get to the root of this underlying fear so you can internalize that you are lovable and you do deserve lasting love with a great man. (And reread the section on how to stop stressing over your relationship from Chapter 7!)

When It Gets Too Intense, He Will Pull Back

Another likely reason is that he's just freaking out a little bit because things are getting more serious. Many guys worry that a girl will become the gatekeeper of their social calendar as soon as a commitment is made, and they will have to say goodbye to watching football with the guys on Sunday, playing sports, and engaging in every other activity they enjoy. Maybe it sounds stupid and irrational, but it's a real fear for most guys.

A lot of guys have that one friend with a possessive, needy girlfriend he has to check in with every five minutes, and he can't do anything fun. Just that could be enough to scare your guy away, at least for a little bit.

When you give him the space and opportunity to maintain his own life and do what he likes to do, this fear dissipates. Don't stand in the way or make him feel guilty or tell him what he should be doing. Encourage him to be who he wants to be and do what he wants to do, and make sure you do the same. A guy may not always ask for space, but he will be grateful anytime it's granted to him. Giving space isn't an issue if your focus is on making your life an amazing place without needing him to make it that way for you.

When he has time to do his thing, either by himself or with his guy friends, he has the chance to recharge an important part of himself. And when he's fully charged, that's when you're going to find him the most attractive. That's when he's going to be that ideal man that you want. And the same goes for women. Women need to recharge their "woman batteries" too, by doing girly stuff with their friends. As a woman, you should never deny a man his time to recharge. This will also benefit you, so everyone wins!

No matter what his reasons for needing space, try not to take it personally and don't harbor resentment towards him over it. Yes, I know you would prefer he talk to you about whatever is going on, but the fact that he doesn't want to is just a sign of how much he cares about you…he cares what you think so much that he doesn't want to come across as weak in your eyes. Try to maintain warm, positive feelings towards him and use the time to focus on yourself and do things that make you feel good.

If you feel really hurt by him taking space, and it's eating away at you, bring it up to him. Just be sure to do it in a loving way, not in an accusatory or attacking way, because that will just make things worse. In the end, remember that when a man needs space, it may have little, if anything, to do with you: He may be stressed out, he may have emotional needs that aren't being met, he may be reacting to clinginess on your part, or he may be worried about losing his freedom. In any of these cases, there are things you can do to reassure him. Focus on those things, and his need for space will no longer be frightening or nerve-wracking. Instead it will be an opportunity to give him something he needs to be his best self.

When He Indirectly Tells You He Needs Space

After about a month of dating, Kara and Mark started spending *all* their time together. They had sleepovers six nights a week and spent every single weekend together. Kara was flattered by the fact that Mark wanted to spend so much time with her and didn't see it as an issue. After a few months of this routine, something funny started to happen. Every few days Mark would say something like, "You know, it isn't good that we spend so much time together, we really should only do sleepovers 3-4 nights a week," Kara usually wouldn't know how to react to this, but it made her feel hurt and rejected.

She was also confused. Mark was the one who initiated all the sleepovers. He was the one always begging to see her. She didn't understand what she could possibly be doing wrong—she was just doing what he wanted. Sometimes when this happened, it would result in a fight, other times just passive-aggressive pouting on her part, but she would always agree and say yes, they did spend too much time together, and a few nights apart would be nice. Then there would be a week of less time spent together, but the following week they were back to spending every night together. He always initiated and she accepted, and like clockwork every few weeks he would express his concern and doubts.

Their relationship became fraught with problems and soon they were always fighting. The only times things were good were when she was able to maintain firm boundaries and take a few nights off. She even did her own thing over an entire weekend and went away with friends, something that had never happened in the eight months they'd been together. But sadly, she would always fall back into the same routine, and it was almost like Mark resented her for being so available…even though *he* was the one initiating.

So what was the problem? Even though men need space and freedom, they don't always know how to go about getting it. When you develop a pattern in the relationship of spending so much time together very early on, a man may also feel that this is what is expected of him, and he's afraid that scaling back will cause problems. Also, Mark did want to spend time with Kara, he loved going to sleep with her and waking up with her in the morning.

But deep down he was also feeling a need for space and freedom. Another issue he had was the fact that they weren't even engaged, yet they were acting like a married couple. This is something else he would bring up to her that she just didn't know how to handle. Essentially, he felt like they were moving too fast, but he didn't know how to find the brakes so he was dragging her along for the ride.

When the terms of a relationship get confusing, a man will oftentimes not know how to respond. This is where you need to take the controls and hit the reset button. Mark was clearly (OK maybe not clearly, but the message was coming across loud and clear in the subtext) telling Kara that he wanted her to do her own thing, but she didn't have the strength to do it.

Why Men Lose Interest

Here is a situation many girls have experienced. You meet a guy and feel the proverbial spark. Numbers are exchanged, flirty texting ensues, and eventually you go on a date…and it's amazing!

The chemistry is strong, you connect, you have fun. You go out again and it's another ace in the hole. Now you start to get really excited…could this be it? Maybe you hang out a few more times and it goes well, but then something changes.

Either you notice that he starts to pull away and seems less engaged (commonly known as "the fade-away"), or he just vanishes (a phenomenon known as "ghosting"). You feel completely blindsided and shell-shocked.

What went wrong?

Here is why this situation is so confusing. When a woman loses interest in a guy after a few dates, she can usually pinpoint the reason. Maybe he was too desperate, not intellectually stimulating, too quiet, too loud, too boring, too boisterous—she usually knows exactly what it is that turned her off and can give a reason if asked as to why she doesn't want to continue dating him.

It's not always like this for guys. A guy can go on a few amazing dates with a girl and find himself suddenly and inexplicably put off by her. Whereas he was previously texting her throughout the day and feeling a strong desire to see her…he now has no desire to contact her whatsoever. This can be as baffling for guys as it is for girls. When asked, many guys will say they don't know why they were suddenly turned off…they just were.

So why does this happen? Is it really out of the blue without cause or provocation? No, there is a reason. The reason it's so hard to pinpoint and articulate is because it's extremely subtle.

During the first few dates with a new guy, your vibe is typically pretty laid-back and easygoing. You want to explore the possibilities with him and see what he's all about. It starts out light and fun, and it's about connecting and enjoying each other's company. After a few great dates with a seemingly great guy, most women can't help but get excited about the possibilities. They think of where the relationship might go and they start to invest in a fantasy future.

When this happens, you are no longer in the here and now, seeing the situation for what it is. Instead, your mind is focusing on what it could be and that's when the problem starts. You become attached to this fantasy future and then you can't help but stress over it and worry about losing it (even though it's not something you ever really had!) Then your fears and insecurities rise to the surface and seep into your interactions with him.

You begin interacting with the thoughts in your head rather than with the person in front of you. Rather than trying to learn who he is and what he's about, you look at his behavior and the things he says as a means to measure how he feels about you…and whether you're getting closer or further away from your goal of having a relationship with him.

Most guys can intuitively sense when a woman is reacting to them as an object rather than a person, when she is using him as a means to fill a void within herself.

Guys typically don't operate this way in relationships and he can't fully understand what happened to turn this seemingly happy, cool girl into an unpleasant, emotionally-reactive, reassurance-seeking mess.

Why Do We Do This?

All anyone really wants is to feel OK, and most of us don't. When a woman worries and needs constant reassurance, it comes from feeling "I am not OK" and the feeling beneath that is fear. What makes it so destructive is that it's not an overwhelming, gripping fear; it's a vague feeling of unease. It's so quiet and subtle you may not even realize it's there. You know how sometimes you'll go to take a sip of water and find you literally can't stop chugging? You didn't even realize you were thirsty, it was only when you began to quench your thirst that you realized how potent it was. That's kind of what's at play here.

It's tough for people to nail down the source of feeling not OK, but they unconsciously latch onto things that will elim- inate this feeling, usually through reassurance or trying to make situations come about that they feel will make them happy and finally grant them relief. This inevitably impacts your vibe, you become a parasite of sorts, and everyone you come into contact with is simply a means to an end.

When you meet a guy who makes you feel OK, your need for that feeling becomes overwhelming and you latch on forcefully. You may not even realize you're doing it; it's not something you express outright. But it's there and it comes across, even in the slightest ways. It changes your vibe and your energy, and guys feel this.

At this point, instead of him feeling like he's connecting with you, he feels like you're trying to get something out of him. Maybe it's reassurance or validation, or maybe just more of the feeling of being OK.

Guys don't know exactly what it is, but suddenly their instincts are telling them to get away. This usually occurs at the point where the woman could no longer keep the act up. Maybe she's trying to appear cool and go-with-the-flow, but in her mind she's already thinking of ways to turn a relationship that's really nothing at this point into something. From that point forward, it's not easygoing and natural, it's her measuring if she is getting closer or further from her goal.

Everyone recognizes when someone has an agenda. It's just something our intuition picks up on, and it immediately puts us off. Think about how you feel when someone approaches you and tries to sell you something. Your first instinct is typically to get far away from them. It doesn't matter how nice and friendly they are, you can't trust them because you know they want something out of you.

That's the switch guys feel. It's the shift from things being easy and fun to agenda-driven. When the woman feels like she's getting closer to her goal, she's happy and elated. When something happens that makes her feel like she is moving further away, she is gripped by that, "My world is falling apart" feeling and may try to seek reassurance from the guy, either outright or subtly.

You Can't Force Love

When you take a relationship that is brand new and start thinking that it's something, or try forcing it to be more than it is, it's game over. Your vibe will become man-repelling and before long, he'll be gone and you will be left baffled, analyzing what exactly you did to drive him away. But you won't ever find the answer, because it isn't concrete and measurable.

This is one of the main differences between men and women when it comes to relationships. Men are more in the moment and are able to comfortably enjoy a situation for what it is as it is. Women are always looking for ways to improve the relationship and push it forward. It's not that one gender has it right and the other has it wrong. There needs to be a balance between enjoying the present and comfortably laying the foundation for a future. It just can't be done forcefully.

The best relationships are the ones that unfold organically with two people bringing their best selves to the table and discovering who the other person is and developing an appreciation for that person. It's not about using the other person to gain status or self-esteem or security. A relationship can give you these things, but that's a by-product, not the goal.

This is essentially the difference between a healthy relationship and a toxic relationship. A healthy relationship is one where two people feel fulfilled by their individual lives and let that joy and sense of fullness spill into their relationship. They each bring something to the table and can comfortably give and receive. A dysfunctional relationship is when one or both people believe the other person can "give them" something or that there's something to "get" from the other person.

So what's the solution? If you just enjoy life and engaging with him and make nothing of it, your vibe will still be enjoyable to be around and he will continue hanging out with you. When he feels good around you, he'll want to be around you. When he feels like you're trying to get something out of him, he will want nothing to do with you. It really is as simple as that. Also, don't look at his level of interest as life or death. Understand and accept that you'll be totally fine if things don't work out, so there is nothing to worry about.

I also want to add that this isn't the *only* reason a man will lose interest; it's just the most common and most misunderstood one. The problem is that most people don't accurately define what the problem is. It gets written off as the woman being too available and not making the guy chase her. That's not really what's at play here. Being available isn't the issue, the issue is really not being present. It's an issue that comes from seeking validation through a relationship rather than in your life.

It is also worth noting that sometimes two people can be happy and satisfied in their lives and just not be a match. Compatibility can't be forced or created, and a lack of it can't be ignored. If you're incompatible, it will come to the surface eventually, and a relationship can't last without a foundation of fundamental compatibility.

The winning strategy when it comes to love is to bring your best self to the table and not to stress over your relationship. Instead, trust that if it's right it will work out, and if it's not right you'll be free to move towards something that is the right match for you.

Why Guys Disappear and How to Deal

Here's a scenario that might sound familiar. You're seeing a guy for a little while, it could be weeks or maybe months. You text a lot, hang out, have fun, things seems to be moving along swimmingly, and a relationship seems like it's just around the corner.

Then poof…he's gone. Vanished without a trace.

He might do the slow fade-out, meaning he stops initiating contact and when you reach out to him he takes hours or days to reply. This goes on for a while until you take the unfortunate hint. Or he "ghosts" and just disappears. He doesn't reach out and he doesn't reply when you contact him.

When this happens, the girl becomes desperate to know why. Maybe his vanishing act came after a period of him pulling away. Or maybe it came suddenly, out of the blue. It doesn't matter, it means the same thing: he's not into you and doesn't see this relationship going anywhere. Maybe he met someone else or maybe he just had an epiphany. The damage is done, there's nothing you can do, so don't torture yourself over it.

I've been there, so believe me I know how awful it feels. Like the absolute worst.

Like many women, my reaction was a mix of rage and indignation. *Why can't he just be a man and break up with me to my face?? What a coward!*

So why doesn't he just say this to your face? Because it's an uncomfortable conversation to have and he doesn't want to have it. Simple as that. Also, men just aren't as equipped to handle emotions and emotional situations as well as women are, so they avoid them.

Girls don't like having the breakup conversation and guys absolutely *despise* it. Most men would rather walk over a bed of burning hot coals than tell a girl to her face that they're not into her. So they ghost. And most of the time, they will reason that the girl is probably on the same page so there is no need to reach out. They tell themselves that she must know this isn't going to work out, and calling and telling her something she already knows would just be silly, so that's the end of that.

OK so now that we know why, let's talk about what to do to help you move on to greener pastures.

1. Don't Reach out to Him

Under any circumstance! He may have left you, but don't let him take your dignity with him. Girls will come up with all kinds of deluded reasons to explain why they absolutely must initiate contact. *I just need closure! I want to know how he's doing! I HAVE to tell him about this really funny thing that happened!*

He stopped initiating contact with you because he is no longer interested in you. The sooner you realize and accept this, the better off you'll be. Remember, if he wanted to see you or speak to you, he would.

2. Don't Take It Personally

When a guy disappears, it's almost inevitable to feel a flood of self-doubt. *What did I do wrong? Why wasn't I good enough?*

You didn't do anything wrong. You are "good enough" to have the relationship you want with a man you want, this guy just wasn't it. I know plenty of gorgeous, smart, funny, successful, amazing women who have had the vanishing act pulled on them, and it didn't make them any less gorgeous, smart, amazing, etc.

A guy can lose interest for any number of reasons. Sometimes he feels put off by your vibe (as we discussed in the previous section), other times it has nothing to do with you. The worst possible thing you can do is take it personally and start beating yourself up over it. This will eat away at your self-esteem and repel any new potential suitors who might come along. Try to keep your ego out of your relationships as much as possible. Your relationship status should never determine your worth as a person.

3. Stay Busy

As with most painful experiences…only time will heal. And as time works its magic, the best thing you can do is stay as busy as possible. Immerse yourself in work, spend time with friends, check out a cool new bar or museum, try out a new exercise class. Keep your schedule jam-packed so there isn't a crack for him to slip right in. And do not check up on him on Facebook, Twitter, Instagram, or any other social media portal.

If you feel the need to check up on him, go look at funny YouTube videos or call a friend. Staying busy and keeping your life fun and fulfilling will also have positive long-term results and will put you in a better position to attract an even better guy.

Now let's all breathe a sigh of relief that those Houdinis did us the courtesy of finding something better!

Remember This

Sometimes men pull away because they're turned off by something you did, and other times when they withdraw it has nothing to do with you. Either way, the best thing you can do is gracefully pull back and let him do what he needs to do. Use that time to focus on what you need as well."

10

How to Communicate

Healthy relationships...Let's not forget it's You and Me vs. The Problem...NOT You vs. Me.

– Steve Maraboli

Communication is the gateway to an amazing relationship. Unfortunately, it's not always the easiest skill to master. In relationships, both romantic and not, it's not so much what you say, it's the way you say it that makes all the difference. Saying the right words in the right way can lead to a closer connection and increased happiness for both people. Saying things in the wrong way can cause massive fights and mounting resentments.

Communicating well during a heated argument is an art of its own, but what really makes all the difference is the day-to-day communications. It's about how you express your needs, show your appreciation, and express love to your partner in the way he most feels it.

Getting a Man to Do Anything for You

Here is a common relationship scenario that any woman who has ever been in a relationship has most likely experienced.

Your guy isn't doing something you want him to do (and know he's capable of doing). You call him out on it and he withdraws, and not only does he not do the thing you asked, he may even do the opposite.

For instance, let's say a guy was a texting machine in the beginning of the relationship, but then as the relationship progressed, the number of daily texts started to drop.

The girl really misses the good old days of constant texts. She knows he's capable of it, she's unhappy that he no longer does it, so in her mind the logical thing to do is say something to him about it.

So she says, "Why don't you text me all the time like you used to?" thinking that she's sending her message loud and clear...and she is, right?

Well, when she says this to a guy, he feels like a failure. He feels like he isn't living up to her expectations and as a result, he feels defeated.

A man wants to give and provide for you, men are just wired that way.

When he feels like he's incapable of meeting your needs, he feels like a failure as a man.

It may not even be conscious on his part. It's a feeling that emerges beneath the surface and manifests as him withdrawing or continuing to do the thing that bothers you.

So what's the solution?

It's pretty simple and if you can master it, you will never again feel frustrated by your man.

The solution is to *empower* him by encouraging the kinds of behaviors on his part that make you happy and make you love and desire him, rather than demanding that he be a certain way and pointing out the ways in which he's failing to make you happy.

If a man feels that his girl respects, appreciates and can happily receive what he has to give, he will do anything to keep her happy.

So how do you do this? Well this is the tricky part. It isn't about something you should say or do in order to get him to do what you want. That's just manipulative, and if that's the place you're coming from, he'll sense it and it will make things worse.

The kind of woman who gets the unwavering attention and affection so many other women crave from their partners is the one who is in a good place emotionally.

She doesn't demand anything from him and she doesn't need anything from him.

Instead, she sees and appreciates him for who he is, and she is OK if there are times when he doesn't do exactly what she wants. This, in turn, makes him want to go above and beyond for her.

When a woman is unstable, or carrying hurt/pain/insecurities, she will pressure her man to act a certain way in order to feel better about the situation, not because she actually needs him to text five times a day.

If a woman is holding onto these pains and fears, she isn't coming from a place of love, she's coming from a place of needing to control her man and the relationship or her self-esteem will suffer.

Men never ever respond well to demands, and they want to be wanted, not needed.

The point I'm making (and have been making throughout this book) is that it's vital to work on yourself and get to a strong place internally, a place where you can receive what he has to give, not a place that makes you feel empty and alone when he doesn't do every single thing you want exactly the way you want him to.

Emotional development takes work, so here is a helpful way to know if you're coming from a place of neediness so you can hopefully begin to work on it.

When you feel disappointed/frustrated/angry by something your guy is doing and you try to force him to change, you should ask yourself if you're doing it for you or for him.

For instance, if you want your guy to be more emotionally supportive, ask yourself if you want this because it would be beneficial for him in his life to be more sensitive, or is it because you need it in order to feel more confident in the relationship because you're feeling unstable or insecure and need his reassurance in order not to feel abandoned?

Going back to our previous example, why is it that you want him to text more often?

Is it because you feel that being in constant communication will strengthen the relationship and make it better for both of you, or is it because you're unsure about his feelings and use his texts as a barometer for how he feels?

If you can step back and examine your true motivations

for wanting something out of your guy, you will gain important insight into yourself.

You will also create space to see the situation more objectively and will be better able to act without pushing your guy away.

The Magic Formula

When it comes to communicating with men, there is a simple magic formula that is so powerful it can literally transform your entire relationship into one that is happier and more filled with love than you ever imagined.

I was talking to a friend the other day who is having a hard time with her husband. She doesn't feel he is affectionate enough with her and wishes he would give her compliments and words of affirmation more often. She said every time she brings it up, he gets defensive and angry and counters by saying he does do those things for her and he's trying his best, but when she doesn't acknowledge him for it and instead keeps telling him he isn't doing enough, it makes him want to stop trying.

This is a common issue any woman in a relationship is bound to run into. The reason is that we often don't know how to speak in a language that our man will hear and understand. And that's because it's a tough thing to do, especially when we're feeling hurt or upset by his behavior.

The truth is, men are easy creatures. It's very easy to get your guy to treat you the way you want to be treated, you just have to go about it the right way. If you go about it the wrong way, he will become the most stubborn, difficult person you have ever encountered.

And the right way to communicate with a man is as follows…

Whenever you need something from your guy, frame it using this formula:

Praise→ Request→ Thanks.

Here are some examples:

- "You are such a great guy and I know you wouldn't do something to intentionally hurt me, because you never do things to intentionally hurt me. I really would appreciate it if you could be a little more supportive and encouraging because this is a stressful time for me. Thank you so much for always being there and always trying, I really appreciate it."

- "You are so loving and do so much for me. I really love it when you show me affection and give me compliments. If you could be more affectionate, it would make me feel even more loved by you. I know that being affectionate and complimentary doesn't come naturally to you, so thank you so much for trying and for realizing this is important to me."

- "You are such a go-getter and are so amazing at your job, and the success you have achieved is incredible. I know you're very busy at work, but I would love it if you could try to call or text me more often during the workday, because it makes me feel good when I hear from you. I really appreciated it the other day when you took the time to call me even though you had back-to-back meetings. I noticed it, and it made me feel really good that you took time out of your day to check in with me."

You get the gist. It sounds simple on paper, but I know that when you're angry with him, or hurt, it can be really difficult to summon this sort of compassion. Instead, you may subconsciously want to hurt him back and make him feel really bad because he's making you feel bad.

You need to realize that this approach gets you absolutely nowhere. When you frame things like, "Why don't you ever compliment me/appreciate me/support me/call me? I do everything for you and you can't even do the little things I need, and it's not fair!" his defenses will immediately go up, and nothing you say will penetrate. Instead, he'll say that you don't appreciate him, you don't respect him, you're being unreasonable ..which will make you even more upset and cause you to lash out even more ..which will make him even more defensive and accusatory ..and the resentments, hurt, and anger will continue to mount.

In relationships, most women primarily need to feel loved and cared for while most men need to feel appreciated and significant. Feeling significant is tied to feeling like a winner, which is the number-one need for a man both in life and in love. When you focus on what he's doing wrong and make him the bad guy, he feels like he's failing you, and this will make him less motivated to give you what you want. It's the same as when he isn't doing things that make you feel loved, and then you're less loving towards him, or less inclined to show him appreciation.

Relationships aren't a quid-pro-quo exchange; they're not about keeping score or going tit-for-tat. When you take that approach you will always lose. Maybe you're totally right, maybe he isn't affectionate enough for you, but although proving this with a list of examples may win you the battle, you will lose the war because your relationship will suffer.

Men are highly, *highly* sensitive when it comes to criticism and rejection. He doesn't want to feel like a bad guy who is incapable of making you happy. The one thing he wants more than anything in a relationship is to see you smile. So when you have an issue to bring up with him, it's also important that you don't frame it as him being the problem. For example, saying something like, "You're so insensitive and I can't deal with it!"

Again, making him feel bad about himself won't get you anywhere. It's also not a nice thing to do to someone you love. Instead, you can say, "I'm really stressed right now and that's not your fault; I just don't handle stress very well, and in stressful times I need some extra love and support from you." That is so much better than saying, "Can't you see how stressed I am? Why can't you just support me instead of being so difficult?!"

Believe me, I know how difficult it can be to do this when you're feeling hurt or overwhelmed or stressed. If you can't summon an ounce of love or compassion in that moment, then don't address the issue until you are able to get out of that emotional whirlpool. This could take ten minutes, a few hours, or a few days. However long it takes, try not to bring up the issue until you are able to do it from a place of equanimity.

Emotions can be contagious. If you come at him from an

angry, accusatory place, he will feel defensive and then will also be angry and accusatory, and then nothing will get resolved and no one will be happy.

In a relationship, it's always important to try to see the good. There will always be some bad because no one is perfect, not him and not you. What you choose to focus on is what makes all the difference.

You can choose to dwell on his flaws and all the little ways he isn't making you happy, or choose to see the good, to appreciate him for the things he is doing, which in turn will make him want to do even more. It's like those artsy photographs where there is a beautiful flower in focus and everything else is blurry. In relationships, try to adjust your lens so the flower is in focus and shines brighter than the other stuff.

Remember, all it takes is Praise→ Request→ Thanks. If you frame what you need in that way, you will notice he becomes a whole new man, and your relationship will become a much happier, more loving place.

Rules to Obey When You Argue

Conflicts are a built-in part of any relationship. No two people, no matter how perfectly matched, will get along in perfect harmony at all times. One of the greatest accomplishments in my relationship with my husband is not that we never argue, but that we argue so well (which actually means that we're good at resolving our conflicts).

This was not the case earlier in our relationship, especially not when we were engaged. Back then if we went two days without a fight it was cause for celebration. We used to fight bad and dirty. Petty disagreements would spiral into all-out war. It wasn't pretty, and there were times I wondered if we were going to make it. Sometimes in the midst of an argument it felt like we were speaking two totally different languages, completely unable to comprehend what the other was trying to say.

One of the most essential skills for a couple to master is learning how to argue well. We both had to do some work to get to a place where we could disagree peacefully, but ever since we got married we hardly ever argue. When we do, we're able to resolve it in record time, and afterwards our relationship is usually even stronger than before. That's the thing about conflict: when handled right, your relationship can strengthen. When done wrong, you each can start holding onto resentment and this can erode any happy, loving feelings within the relationship.

So let's talk about the right way to argue. First, it's important to remember that arguments are a chance to grow, and that you and your partner are fighting for the same cause (to reach a place of love and harmony). He's not your enemy and you're not his, so above all else make sure to enter into the interaction from a place of unity so it's each of you facing a conflict together, not each of your pitted against the other.

1. Respond Instead of Reacting

Learning the distinction between responding and reacting will help your relationship enormously, and it's also a very valuable life skill.

When you respond, you are in control; you get to weigh your options and determine how you feel and how you would like to handle the situation. You don't blame the other person for "making" you feel a particular way, because you are in the drivers seat.

When you react, they have complete control. You may say things you don't mean, feel things you don't want to feel. You go on instinct and may regret how you reacted. Reacting rarely takes things in a positive direction. Your knee-jerk reaction may be anger and indignation, or you may try to get back at the other person.

Learning to respond instead of react sounds great in theory, but it can be really difficult in practice, especially when things are heated. You are really going to have to gain control of your mind to do this right.

Just remind yourself that you get to choose how to respond to what's happening; you don't need to be controlled by your immediate reactions, which may only be manifestations of anger in the moment, anger that will soon dissipate. When you cave to these fleeting emotions, the conflict will only continue to escalate.

I don't expect you or anyone to stop having negative thoughts. Even after years of practice I can't do that, and there's no sense in beating yourself up over there. What any person *can* do is choose not to *feed into the negativity.* Even if you have a negative thought or negative initial reaction, just accept that it happens and make a solemn decision not to feed into it. When you can do that, then the rest of the good habits will take hold and conflict patterns will dissolve.

2. Take a Step Back

This is part of learning to respond instead of react. If things start to get really heated, tell your partner that now just isn't a good time to talk about whatever the issue is and you'd like to discuss it later. In the meantime, you should take a walk, go to the gym, or just go someplace where you can be by yourself to let things settle down and gain some more clarity and perspective.

In moments of anger we all kind of turn into two-year-olds throwing a tantrum. We can't see beyond our own pain and the anguish of the moment. Toddlers can be perfectly happy one minute, laughing and giggling and everything is great, but then something happens and it's like the whole world is ending. All they can feel is the pain of the moment and a crushing disappointment because the happiness from two minutes before no longer exists.

In a heated exchange, you might totally forget that this person in front of you is someone you love, someone you're sharing a life with, someone you admire. All you see is that he's being stubborn or difficult and making your life hard, and all the good within him disappears. Maybe he is being a huge jerk and maybe he does deserve your wrath, but conversations had in moments of anger or extreme emotion rarely go in a positive direction. Instead, things typically escalate and worsen.

Like I said earlier, you're on the same team, and the goal is to get along and reestablish that connection you share. As soon as you step away from a situation, you might see things in a whole new light; something that seemed like the end of the world a few minutes earlier might not be that big of a deal.

3. Get to the Root of the Problem

The reason a lot of couples get into the cycle of endless arguing is because they don't address the root of the problem. Instead they argue about trivial things instead of the *real* thing.

One big complaint women have is that their guy doesn't help out at all, and they have to do everything. They may have a fight over him not taking out the garbage or leaving dirty dishes in the sink, but they aren't addressing the core issue. Maybe they'll argue that not taking the garbage out will attract bugs and rodents (a valid argument!) but that isn't the point. The point is the woman most likely feels taken for granted and maybe like her man doesn't care for her. That's what's really going on.

Whenever you have recurring arguments, or find yourself going at it over something that seems trivial, try to uncover what you're really upset about.

4. Don't Fight Dirty

In a moment of anger, it's tempting to jab your opponent between the ribs, but it isn't helpful and will only make things worse! Try not to resort to name-calling, labeling, and attacking to get your point across. Also, stay away from overgeneralization. ("You never do anything for me." "You always leave things lying around.) No one ever *always* or *never* does something, and I'm sure anytime someone used an always or a never on you it was infuriating.

Name-calling is also problematic. Yes, it may have been in

a moment of anger, but once you say it you can't unsay it, and you don't know how it's going to hit your partner and affect him. Instead of "You're such a jerk," you can say, "You were acting like a jerk." Just that small little tweak makes a difference because people always get defensive when they are given a negative label.

Even though your partner might be making you insane, remember that he isn't *all bad.* If he were, you wouldn't be with him (hopefully). He's actually someone you like and love, and we should never intentionally try to hurt the people we care about. That's destructive and can lead to a toxic relationship.

5. Remember That Being Sorry is Better than Being Right

Look, I know what it feels like when you are so frustrated with your partner and basically want to wring his neck because you are so right and he is so wrong. How can he possibly not realize how incredibly stupid and wrong he is and how he makes no sense? And you make so much sense it's insane!

All you want is to prove that you're right because…you are right! And maybe you are. But when you get locked in this kind of battle you both lose because you become opponents; you're fighting against each other, and the other person becomes your enemy. And if you're in a fight, then chances are he thinks you're wrong, and chances are, he's probably right. He's probably a little wrong and a little right, just like you're a little wrong and a little right.

What will get you to a place of understanding and resolution is to not try to win and prove who's right, it's to be sorry that your partner was hurt (even if he was wrong). It sucks to be the first to apologize (and if you're always the first to apologize that is a sign that something is amiss in the relationship, and it should definitely be addressed because not being able to take responsibility is a major red flag). You don't want to apologize; you don't think he deserves it, and maybe he doesn't. But no matter what, no matter how justified you are, you can still be sorry that he is hurt, or sorry that you said something you shouldn't have. Because when you love someone, you don't ever want to hurt him or cause him pain.

In a moment of conflict it may not feel that way, but overall, that's where you're coming from (hopefully, anyway). Trying to prove your case won't get you anywhere. Showing empathy and compassion and owning up to whatever your share in the conflict was will usually get the other person to do the same. Yes, I know it's annoying to be the bigger person, but someone has to do it; otherwise you'll be forever locked in a battle of wills, and no relationship can survive in that state.

You can't win every argument, and some conflicts will never be solved. You just need to respect each other and respect your differences. Part of the reason my husband and I had such a rocky engagement is because we couldn't get there. One big point of contention stemmed from him feeling very uncomfortable with "extravagance." He is much more practical and grounded than I am. I am not a big spender by any means, but I am a bit more liberal with money. That spilled into almost every interaction, especially since weddings can bleed you dry. We clashed over the cost of everything: the furniture we'd buy for our apartment, the items in our registry, the cost of my wedding dress. (He just couldn't understand how one dress could cost so much, and I had to explain that my dress was actually on the cheaper side!)

We were fighting about all these little things, but really the problem was that we weren't respecting the other person's point of view. I thought he was being difficult and annoying for adding to my stress (which, I'll be honest, he was!) and he thought I was a spendthrift and didn't pay attention to budgets. When we got to the root of the issue, we realized that we're just different in this area and we needed to respect those differences. And somehow, we found a way to make it work.

Since we got married, we haven't had a single fight about money. I've learned to respect his mindfulness about budgets and being practical, and he has learned to appreciate that having a nice apartment with nice things really is…nice!

How to Get More Love From Him

I'm going to share the secret to getting more love from your guy and that is…be lovable!

I know, I know, it sounds pretty revolutionary. But here's the thing, I don't think a lot of us realize the kind of energy we're putting out there and into our relationships.

Relationships have a way of bringing all our unresolved crap to the surface. And sometimes, we may unknowingly use our relationship as an emotional dumping ground for everything that's bothering us. We may also take our frustrations out on our partner (the same way we did with our parents when we were younger) because those feelings need to be unleashed somewhere!

It's far easier to get mad at your guy for not being emotionally supportive about how horrible your boss is than to get into a fight with your boss about how mean she is.

I'm not saying you shouldn't ever vent or share your feelings in your relationship. You can and you should, as long as you don't turn personal problems into relationship problems. You need to have a handle on your own life so you don't let negativity from the outside seep into the relationship. The way to do this, for example, is to vent about what's going on, then lovingly thank your guy for listening and do something sweet for him. This will enhance the amount of love in your relationship whereas yelling at him for not being more sympathetic to your situation will just make things worse.

When you allow negativity to seep into your mind and body, you transmit a highly unattractive vibe. I remember a point during my engagement where I was literally my ugliest internal self. Even though I was planning a wedding to get married to the most amazing man I've ever known, I was spouting negativity end to end. I was stressed and overwhelmed (and the roaches!) and I would complain to anyone who would listen, especially my guy. And I was always mad at him for something. Sometimes it was justified, other times I was just taking things out on him.

One night we decided to go out on a date, something we hadn't done in months! I had decided earlier that day to release all my negativity and just enjoy doing something fun for a change. That decision completely changed everything. My guy even noticed something looked different about me when we met up. We had an incredible night and I felt more love and connection than ever before.

At the end of our date I thanked him for being so loving and he replied "Thank you for being so lovable." I was pretty awestruck. That's all it takes? That's how easy it is? And in that moment, a concept I have written about countless times really got hammered in: all a man really needs in a relationship is for the woman he's with to be thoroughly happy.

You can certainly vent to him when you have a lot going on, but it's important to do it in a way where you don't make him feel like the problem and you let him know how much you appreciate having him there to listen.

Men don't always realize that just hearing a woman out serves a purpose and helps her feel better. For example, when you see him after a hard day don't unleash a litany of complaints on him or an itemized list of all the things that went wrong that day, first tell him how happy you are to see him, how it's been a tough day but being with him makes it better. Let him know his presence is the solution in your life, and then you can share what happened with him.

The takeaway message is this: getting angry at your guy for not being as loving as you want will not fill him with loving feelings towards you. What makes him feel loving is when you are lovable.

And now we're going to come full circle. In order to be lovable you must love yourself. There is no other way. And that is at the root of what creates an amazing, happy, loving relationship. That should be your focus more than anything else. That is what makes all the difference. And that is what will change everything and open the door to getting the love you've always wanted.

Remember This

Be on the same team as your man; he is your ally, not your adversary. When you have this mindset you will defeat any conflict rather than allowing the conflict to defeat you.

Conclusion

Well we made it to the end, and I hope you enjoyed the journey! I certainly enjoyed going back through the archives and all the content I've written over the years—some from five years ago, some from five weeks ago. Another cool part about going through it all was the realization that I wrote most of these articles while I was living through the experiences I shared with you. All the articles, all that research, and all that investigating brought me where I am today. I was 23 and single as can be when I started A New Mode. Now I'm a tad older and married and a much more refined, savvy, self-aware version of my former self. Of course the journey never ends, there's always so much more to learn. Being married has opened a new door for me in many ways and given me a whole new arsenal of topics to write about, and ANM will keep on evolving with me.

I hope you come onboard and join the ANM community if you haven't yet. You can always find us at anewmode.com but also be sure to subscribe to our mailing list for honest and personal relationship advice from both Eric and me. You can join at anewmode.com/subscribe. You can like us on Facebook (https://www.facebook.com/anmdaily/), like me on Facebook (https://www.facebook.com/sabrinaalexisanm/), follow us on Instagram (@anewmode), or send me an e-mail with your thoughts and feedback (Sabrina@anewmode.com).

I hope you feel clear and empowered, and that you get and keep that love you've always wanted. Stay in touch!

Lots of love,
Sabrina Alexis

P.S. You should now be equipped with everything you need to know to find and keep love that lasts. We covered a lot in this book, and I want all the material to really stay with you, to penetrate and make the kind of difference that will allow you to get and keep a happy, loving, mutually fulfilling relationship. So here is a little refresher course before we say goodbye. I've pulled the most important information from each chapter and elaborated on why it's such a life-changer.

———————

If you find yourself struggling with a situation that you don't know how to handle, but don't have time to reread this entire book, use this cheat sheet to get you quickly back on track!

Everything You Needs to Know If You Want Love That Lasts: Cheat Sheet

1. Choose Wisely

I spent far too many years wondering why my relationships always fell apart and I couldn't get anything to last. The answer was so obvious I felt like a fool for failing to see it all along: I was choosing the wrong men. I was choosing the men who wouldn't or couldn't give me what I wanted. When I finally wised up and started dating with more of a purpose, dating with the aim of finding something long lasting instead of dating around just for the sake of dating around, I cultivated a new mantra: I want a partner, not a project.

When it hit me it changed my life. I had spent so many years trying to cure these damage cases who would have been terrible lifelong partners! What a colossal waste of time and energy. I didn't want someone I had to fix. Yeah, the challenge could be invigorating, but life is exhausting enough, why make it even more complicated? You need to date selectively. You need to have a firm sense of what you want and need and don't compromise…no matter how sexy and mysterious he is!

2. Love is Amazing…but It Isn't a Fantasy

Love won't make all your pain and problems go away. It won't erase the memory of all your old hurts and wounds, it won't give you a healthy sense of self-esteem, and it won't open the gates of everlasting happiness and bliss. Love can enhance your life in many ways (healthy love, that is), but it will never be perfect. There is no such thing as a perfect partner or a perfect relationship.

This one took me a while to fully grasp because like many women, I fell for the popular ideology our culture perpetuates about love. I thought that with the right person, it would all just work out and everything would be amazing. I thought love was enough. But it isn't. It's also about timing (it has to be the right time for both people), fundamental compatibility, similar goals, and emotional maturity. Love can be a beautiful, transformative thing, but not in a vacuum. A lot of other elements need to align, and you need to accept and embrace the fact that it will take a bit of work.

3. Sometimes You're the Problem

Being single for an extended amount of time can be for two reasons: you legitimately haven't met the right guy, or you aren't yet the right girl. I dated my husband in high school and we ran into each other countless times over the span of a decade. Our last chance meeting was two months before we actually started dating again. For whatever reason when he saw me that day in Central Park, he wasn't overcome with a desire to ask me out. Then two months later he was. By our second date he knew I was "the one."

So what changed? Nothing changed about me physically, but I'd spent that entire summer really working on myself. I focused on friends and fun and getting to the root of some of my longstanding issues. I'm not saying this is exactly why he asked me out, but I just don't think it's a coincidence that once I was in this amazing, empowered place, he plopped back into my life (and is now stuck in it for the long haul!) I'm not saying it's your fault, but we could all stand some self-improvement; making some tweaks can help turn us into our best selves, the self that is capable and worthy of attracting the love we've always wanted.

4. Stop Wasting Time!

Oh what I would do to get back some of the time I've wasted over the years on total losers. If he won't be your boyfriend, if he won't commit, if he treats you badly, if he doesn't appreciate you, if he only appreciates you for sex and can't be bothered when you're fully clothed, forget him. It seems so obvious, yet so many of us fail in this area. Why does it happen?

Essentially, a lot of us are programmed to view ourselves as the problem. We think if only we were better, if we tried harder, if we gave more, then everything would work out. When you make yourself the problem, you can stay stuck in a dead-end relationship for years. Forget the wasted time, think about what that does to your self-esteem. I spent a year obsessing over a guy that I never actually dated! OK, we went on two dates, then he ended it saying he didn't think we were "right for each other," but I couldn't let it go. We would still hang out, still hook up, and each time I would be filled with a renewed sense of hope...until it would all come crashing down and I would once again be left sad and disappointed, wondering what I was doing wrong and why he didn't want to be with me.

But I wasn't the problem, the problem was that he didn't want to be with anyone because he had major commitment issues to overcome. So yes I know I said sometimes you're the problem, but if you're in a dead-end relationship, he's the problem (or rather, the relationship as a whole is problem) and your best bet is to just move on.

5. Everyone Makes Mistakes

When I talk about mistakes women make in relationships, a lot of women will get hyper defensive and say I'm blaming them and it's not their fault because all men are jerks. That's one way to look at things, but it's not a very productive, helpful way to look at things.

The fact is we all need to understand how relationships work: the dynamics at play, what sets the foundation for an amazing relationship, why some last, and why others don't. It requires being open to the idea that you may be doing things wrong, and that's OK! The biggest relationship mistake that I see being committed, and I was once a major offender, is being too needy and expecting way too much out of a man and a relationship.

No relationship will give you everything. You need to realize fulfillment comes from you, and it precedes being in a relationship. You can't expect a relationship to make you happy, especially when you have no idea how to find happiness on your own,

6. Self-Love is Everything

What keeps us in bad relationships isn't that all men are jerks or that relationships are so hard or that we're unworthy or that all the good guys are taken. What keeps us in bad relationships is low self-esteem. When you don't value yourself, you will accept and even welcome people who don't value you into your life. You won't see how wrong this is, how unacceptable this is. If you treat yourself badly, you will accept bad treatment from others. Self-love always comes before healthy romantic love.

I never quite realized this one. Instead I had it backwards, I thought once I found a man to love me, then I too would love myself. But I chased after emotionally unavailable damage cases who, of course, were incapable of giving me love. And even if they had been able to give me love, I wouldn't have been able to receive it because I didn't love myself. The subconscious is always looking to prove itself right. If deep down you feel unlovable, then you will go after men who can't love you. Like attracts like. This is key! If you want someone emotionally stable and healthy, someone who is confident and can give and receive love freely, then you also need to be that kind of person. Whether you're single or in a relationship, you have to always focus on being your best possible self.

7. The Chase is Nonsense!

OK not total nonsense, it does kind of work. But it isn't sustainable! The chase creates the illusion of confidence and leaves enough uncertainty to create the illusion of chemistry. Everything feels more dramatic and exciting when we don't know how the other person feels. But a relationship isn't built on uncertainty. Yes, that can galvanize things, it can rouse interest, but you need something real in order for that interest to remain and deepen.

I used to be a master at the chase. I could easily lure a guy in and spark his interest, but I could never keep it. And I never understood why. The reason, I believe, is that in the beginning I would always hold myself back just a bit. I would start off a little scared (probably because the boy before had burned me) and that came across as being coy.

Men are the opposite. In the beginning they usually come on full force. They see an opportunity and they want to grab it. This begins as the perfect combination; he gets to pursue with all his might, and she makes it a little tough. But eventually she (or me) will give in, will get excited, will make it easier on him because she likes him. But if she isn't coming from the right place, if she's a little insecure and needy, if she craves his validation and approval, if she makes it all about him...then he's gone.

This is why the chase doesn't work. Real relationships require being real, being present, being vulnerable. And they demand that both people be in good places emotionally, otherwise things will quickly unravel or become toxic.

8. Men and Women Fall in Love Differently

They also need different things in a relationship. Men primarily need to feel appreciated for who they are and what they have to give. He needs to feel like a winner. If he doesn't, then he won't want to be in the relationship for very long. You'll notice in most breakups and divorces that the guy says the reason it ended is he no longer felt appreciated, he felt like he couldn't make her happy, like she was always harping on him about something. Men need to feel like the man, they need to be respected for what they provide (this does not only mean material items). Find any man who is unhappy in his relationship and ask him why, and his answer will fall under the umbrella of this concept every time.

9. Men Lose Interest for Reasons You Can't See...

There are overt behaviors that push men away, and there are covert ones...the latter causing a lot more confusion than the former! A few months before I started dating my husband I dated a guy I'll call Aaron. We met at a party and instantly hit it off. He was sexy, successful, cool, charming, and absolutely crazy about me. I resisted his advances in the beginning, feeling a little unsure about things because he was two years younger than I was and seemed to still be living like a college kid in a lot of ways, but eventually I stopped analyzing and started to just enjoy. We texted endlessly, went on a few fun dates, and then it hit me...this might really be something!

Then I started to obsess. But what about the fact that he loves to party so much? Can I handle that even though I'm over that phase of my life? And does that mean he won't be ready for marriage? And he's kind of immature...can I live with that? And how will it work between us...our backgrounds are so different. I was busy plugging away mentally, trying to make this relationship work—I was ready to fight for it.

Then we went on another date. I was a little anxious, a little uneasy, and something just changed dramatically. Even though we shared a passionate kiss at the end of the date I knew I wouldn't be hearing from him again. And I was right. And I was also baffled.

What had gone wrong? Well, my vibe had totally changed and it squeezed the life out of the relationship...and it wasn't even an actual relationship yet. It's not totally my fault, the relationship clearly wasn't meant to last, but it still hurt that he could so quickly lose interest when he'd come on so strong at first. Stressing over a relationship usually ruins is. As does getting attached to a certain outcome. When you expect a serious relationship to unfold with a guy you're casually dating, then you lose something if the relationship ends. When you can just go with it, you only have something to gain.

10. It Doesn't Matter What You Say, It's the Way You Say It

I used to be a terrible communicator. No, scratch that. I was able to effectively communicate in certain settings. My direct, no-nonsense, intellectually thought-out and unemotional way of speaking served me well in terms of my career, but it didn't do me many favors when it came to my relationships.

Communication is a huge determining factor in whether a relationship will survive or fail. You have to learn how to speak in a way so the other person hears you, otherwise you're just wasting your breath and getting nowhere.

About the Author

Sabrina Alexis is the co-founder and editorial director of A New Mode and author of the bestselling book *10 Things Every Woman Needs to Know About Men*. Sabrina graduated from Boston University in 2007 with degrees in English and Psychology and has been writing about fashion, beauty, relationships, and wellness ever since. Her work has appeared on numerous leading sites including *Fox News, Glamour, Maxim, The Huffington Post, The Frisky, Your Tango, Elite Daily, Thought Catalog, The Stir, You Beauty, Observer,* and *StyleList*.

She launched A New Mode in 2009 along with Eric Charles and they quickly gained a large following due to their unique relationship content and deep understanding of relationship dynamics.